EVERYDAY
DINNERS

JESSICA MERCHANT

everyday
dinners

REAL LIFE RECIPES TO SET YOUR
FAMILY UP FOR A WEEK OF SUCCESS

RODALE
NEW YORK

Published in the United States by Rodale Books,
an imprint of Random House, a division of Penguin
Random House LLC, New York.
rodalebooks.com

RODALE and the Plant colophon are registered
trademarks of Penguin Random House LLC.

Library of Congress Cataloging-in-Publication Data
Names: Merchant, Jessica, author.
Title: Everyday dinners / Jessica Merchant.
Description: New York : Rodale Books, 2021. | Includes
    index.
Identifiers: LCCN 2020026690 (print) | LCCN
    2020026691 (ebook) | ISBN 9780593137499
    (hardcover) | ISBN 9780593137505 (epub)
Subjects: LCSH: One-dish meals. | Electric cooking,
    Slow. | Pressure cooking. | Quick and easy cooking. |
    LCGFT: Cookbooks.
Classification: LCC TX840.O53 M47 2021 (print) |
    LCC TX840.O53 (ebook) | DDC 641.82--dc23

ISBN 978-0-593-13749-9
eBook ISBN 978-0-593-13750-5

Printed in China

Production Credits: Lacy Caric
Photographer: Jessica Merchant
Photography Assistant: Erin Alvarez
Editor: Dervla Kelly
Designer: Mia Johnson
Production Editor: Serena Wang
Production Manager: Jessica Heim
Composition: Merri Ann Morrell

10 9 8 7 6 5 4 3 2 1

First Edition

ALSO BY JESSICA MERCHANT

The Pretty Dish

Seriously Delish

To all the readers of
How Sweet Eats who sit at my virtual
dinner table every day, thank you.
Let's eat!

contents

introduction

Ever since I was a kid, dinner has been my favorite part of the day. My family sat around the table nearly every night. Even after eating, my parents, my brothers, and I would sit around the table and often laugh hysterically about something that happened that day.

It's so cliché, but it feels like yesterday. I can put myself around that table now. I hear my family laughing, I see what we're eating. I didn't realize the value in that until I was a bit older and it's something I'm thankful for every day.

However! Cooking dinner as an adult and for a family is a totally different experience than enjoying it as a child. Right?

I know. Raise your hand if dinner stresses you out. I've totally been there, and I love cooking dinner each night. As life gets busier than ever, it's hard to set aside time to throw together a nourishing meal after a long day. What should I make? What sounds good? What won't take an hour to make? And can someone come clean the dishes when I'm done? I mean, I'm serious about that last one.

I GET YOU!

See, my mom made dinner nearly every single night when I was growing up. Every single night! Looking back now, as I have two kids of my own (she had three), I'm constantly like, HOW DID SHE DO IT? She did it with such ease and confidence. And knowing what I know now, she probably did it to provide some of that stable comfort that we were so lucky to have as kids in the '90s.

My childhood memories are full of sitting at the kitchen table on weeknights, doing homework while she made dinner. I can still smell her toasting almonds in brown butter to later dump on green beans. I can hear the sizzle of onions in a pot and the sear of her pot roast.

If I wasn't doing my homework at the kitchen table, I'd run into the kitchen and steal a piece of chicken from a paper towel–lined plate where my mom had left browned chicken tenders as she made chicken marsala, her signature dish. She made it at least once a week and would always have to make extra because I'd steal the browned pieces from the plate.

By early evening our house was fragrant with whatever she was cooking for dinner. And by 4 PM I'd know if we were having tacos or pork chops. At midnight on a Friday I'd often smell cloves and pineapple because she'd have a ham in the oven, so we could have freshly sliced meat for sandwiches over the weekend.

My mom was a superhero at the weeknight meal. While we had a small group of meals in rotation (as most families did in the '90s), they were all SO good and none of us had any complaints. My mom would often alternate side dishes and did it so well that it felt like a completely different meal. And most importantly, we sat around the table together every single night. On nights when my dad got home from work late, my mom would even call me out of bed to come sit at the table with everyone.

On very rare occasions when my dad was out of town, she made breakfast for dinner or scrambled egg combination sandwiches that I'd slather with mustard (Does that sound horrifying? They were fantastic!). And still . . . the rest of us all sat at the table together.

But here's the thing. It wasn't the food that I remember the most. Sure, it was delicious and I think of it fondly, often craving that nostalgic comfort. I remember the weekly traditions, like pasta night and taco night. But, at the risk of sounding corny, what happened during and after the meal is what I remember more than what we actually ate.

The simple acts of my parents passing freshly grated Parmesan back and forth or my brother grabbing an extra biscuit were just highlights in the hour (at least) that we sat down together. Sure, the distractions weren't as glaring as they are today. The TV was turned off; if the phone rang, it was ignored. But my mom's process of cooking wasn't stressful or overcomplicated, even if it took an hour some nights.

Unfortunately, our world moves so fast today that I often find myself eating my dinner standing over the pot in the kitchen, trying to get the kids fed first before I sit down. Yet I crave the soothing time it takes to prep a meal in the kitchen, knowing that I'm about to nourish myself and my family, without the anxious rush or digging a hand into the cereal box to satisfy a crunch craving. I want to bring that back. Not just for my own family, which is relatively young and still building traditions, but for you, too.

In our fast-paced world, it's safe to assume that family dinners can't happen like they did back in the day. We're busier, we work more, we have more distractions and a to-do list that is five miles long. But there are certain things we can do to make dinnertime easier, special, and something to look forward to. Whether it's for a family of one, two, or ten.

What you'll find in this book is a compilation of my favorite dinners, ones that I've been making on busy weeknights for years. Ones that are so good that I make them even when I have more than thirty minutes to cook. There are some that can come together with a little prep time each day. There's a hearty meatless section, along with the expected poultry, seafood, beef, and pork sections. I have also included a few of my favorite side dishes at the end, just to help you tie a meal together.

LET ME SHARE THE REAL SECRET: HOW I DO IT.

Nearly every single meal here can be made in thirty minutes or less. There are a few exceptions—for example, I like to use a baked sweet potato here and there—but if you use a few minutes of prep time to bake that potato, you're golden.

Some of my recipes come with extras—whether that be an avocado crema or a five-minute granola sprinkled on top. These are meant to add extra flair and flavor to the dish, and they are often my favorite part of a recipe. But they aren't always a necessity that will make or break the dish.

I cannot stress this enough: Take these recipes and make them your own. If you've had a rough day, use your favorite jarred salsa instead of a quick homemade pico de gallo. If you're out of ingredients to make your own vinaigrette, use your favorite store-bought version.

And perhaps most importantly, let me share the real secret: HOW I DO IT. **Enter . . . my 10-minute meal prep.**

This has seriously changed my life. I know that's dramatic, but hey, it truly has made life easier. And it's not even that big of a deal. To some, it may not seem feasible or even make sense. I get it. Because when we think of "meal prep," we envision the entire meal being cooked or prepared ahead of time, or making four or five lunches for the week ahead.

But that's not what this book is.

I've found what works best for me, as a working mom with little kids running around, as someone who really loves to cook but doesn't want to spend forever in the kitchen, especially on weeknights, and it's precisely this: ten minutes of prep, when and where I can fit it in. Consistently.

The prep is not optional. But it's flexible as long as I'm consistent. The little bits of prep make up magical time in the kitchen. Sometimes this means ten minutes of prep each day. Sometimes this means ten minutes of prep on Sunday morning and ten minutes on Sunday night.

To be honest, I don't LOVE meal planning. I wish that I could live in a world where I made exactly what "sounds good" for dinner every night. After all, I'm a cravings-based person. And that's where I get hung up on meal planning, because what if I'm not in the mood for something later in the week? I don't want to waste food or ingredients, and I especially don't want to waste *time*.

My solution is to plan and shop for three or four meals throughout the week. This way, we usually have a few leftovers, it leaves open spaces for impromptu restaurant visits or takeout and if needed, a fallback of breakfast for dinner.

I promise that it works.

All of the recipes in this book have one or more tips for a ten-minute meal prep. These are the details that make a difference during the hours between 4 PM and 7 PM when everyone is hungry, cranky, tired, and just plain OVER all the things.

There are so many benefits to this.
But the ones that stick out most in our house?

— **WE END UP EATING MORE BALANCED MEALS.**

— **WE END UP EATING MORE VEGGIES.**

— **WE DON'T WASTE INGREDIENTS.**

— **WE HAVE MORE TIME TOGETHER IN THE EVENINGS.**

— **CLEANUP IS EASIER AND QUICKER.**

When I look at that list of benefits, my mind is blown—because it covers so many goals I have for myself and my family. And that means everything.

THE 10-MINUTE MEAL PREP RULE

The key to 10-minute meal prep? **It's all in the little details.** The basics are to **cook, chop, mix, and assemble** in 10-minute increments, when applicable. I'm talking about the little things that we don't consider when making a meal—the things that add on to our entire cook time or mostly, our cleanup time. Tasks like chopping vegetables ahead of time. Whisking together sauces or marinades and storing them in the fridge. Combining spices so we're not bringing out multiple spice jars and leaving them all over the counter when it's time to sit down. Cooking grains for the week. It's prepping these tiny things that have changed everything for me.

Now, I am flexible with my 10 minutes. If I have an extra busy week, for example, then sometimes I WILL do 20 minutes in one day instead of 10 minutes per day. My meal prep rarely involves fully cooking ingredients (with a few exceptions) because most things just don't taste as good to me when they're not freshly cooked.

Throughout this book, you will find tips and tricks for my 10-minute meal prep secrets and what I do to make a meal come together for my family.

Trust me, I never wanted to be a "meal prep" person. Nothing seems more boring to me than twenty containers with nearly the exact same meal in them, for every day of the week. And I don't want to spend 6 hours cooking on Sunday and then another hour cleaning up a huge mess. If you feel the same, I get it. I've gone down the list as to why meal prep won't work for me, over and over again:

- I want variety.
- I get bored.
- I want to eat what I want in the moment.
- I want to eat something fresh.
- I certainly don't want to eat the same thing for lunch every day.
- I don't want to waste hours of my weekend cooking for the week ahead.

See?! I totally get it.

But let me tell you something: I started implementing this strategy 4 years ago and it has made weeknight meals more practical, delicious, and enjoyable! And I do have a few meal-prep secrets that have really changed the game for me and improved many aspects of my life. Before you laugh at me for saying that "studies have shown," let me tell you that studies *have* actually shown (I KNOW) that by removing some everyday decisions in our lives, our brains are more focused. Loosely planning our meals and knowing what we will be eating, and therefore what we have to prep, removes a decision we need to make that day. It totally works for me.

First, I think it's important to gather a list of meals that you really, really love. Meaning that when you eat them often, you still enjoy them. That's why I've created this book! Now, start prepping!

MY 4 MEAL PREP SECRETS

I wash, cut, and store my vegetables.

This is perhaps the biggest thing for me and one of the reasons we have eaten so many veggies in the last few years. A mere five years ago, I didn't even care for vegetables.

After I determine what we're going to eat that week, I prep as many of the vegetables as I can so they are ready to go. This is as simple as washing heads of broccoli, cutting them into florets, and storing them in a resealable bag or dish with a paper towel. In the fridge, they last for days!

When the time comes for that meal, this also allows me to literally dump the broccoli on a baking sheet, add some seasonings, and roast away. It's a no-brainer! It takes me less than ten minutes to prep and is ready to cook in seconds.

I mix up dressings or sauces ahead of time.

Most dressings and sauces can last in the fridge for a few days—in fact, they may even taste better when they've had time to sit.

This allows a weeknight meal to not only have more flavor, but to also come together quickly! No need to drag out multiple ingredients just to make a sauce or dressing.

I marinate meats or veggies ahead of time, if possible.

I often marinate meat a day or two beforehand and sometimes I do the same with vegetables.

For instance, if we're making fajitas, I will often marinate peppers and onions overnight in the fridge. If I'm serving kale salad, sometimes I massage the kale with dressing and let it sit overnight. Definitely saves time when it comes to dinner.

While this book focuses exclusively on dinners, these are tips that I often apply to breakfasts, lunches, and snacks, too.

I don't do just Sunday meal prep.

I want my weekend to truly be a weekend, so the Sunday meal prep thing just doesn't work for me. I spread my meal prep out over a few days and am flexible with my 10 minutes' prep time. If I have an extra-busy week, then sometimes I will do 20 minutes instead in one day and skip the next day's meal prep.

HOW I COOK (AND WHAT YOU SHOULD EXPECT IN MY RECIPES)

I've been cooking long enough that I've mastered my own technique. And while I will talk about this more later, the most important part of cooking, for me, has been using my senses and tasting as I go.

I encourage you to do these same things when cooking, as they will truly teach you how to cook without a recipe, build your confidence, and make recipes your own. You'll increase your mental recipe box, if you will. Dinners, every single day, will be easier for you.

By introducing variety, you will want to cook more. By cooking more, you'll enjoy more dinners at home. And you'll be feeding yourself and your family balanced and nourishing meals and, hopefully, spending more time around the table, connecting with each other.

My confidence in the kitchen has come from following the super simple, basic tricks below.

Pinches of salt and pepper.

I always use kosher salt (Diamond Crystal) and freshly ground black pepper. I include salt and pepper measurements in most recipes for ease and for those who are truly beginners. But I encourage you to taste your food as you go in order to build layers of flavor. This will get easier as you cook more.

Drizzles of olive oil or other appropriate fats.

I make all of my vinaigrettes with extra-virgin olive oil. When cooking with high heat, I use avocado, coconut, grapeseed, or canola oil. Sometimes you need a little extra in the skillet. A drizzle won't hurt!

Splashes of acid.

That sounds a little insane, but what I mean is a spritz of fresh lemon juice or sometimes even a splash of apple cider vinegar. A drop of lemon juice can bring life to a dish. Apple cider vinegar can mimic sherry in soup if you don't have it on hand. Changes everything!

Adding more or less, even when I've followed a recipe exactly.

Finally, this seems like a no-brainer, but I know that many of us are wired to follow a recipe to a T. As you cook more, you'll learn when you can add a little more and when to hold back; you'll make the recipe geared toward your own tastes.

A FEW TIPS ON COOKING WITHOUT A RECIPE

This is kind of funny, since you're holding a book full of recipes. But I have a secret to tell you. And you may not like it. There is only one true way to learn how to cook without a recipe:

YOU MUST COOK OFTEN.

I know for some of you that sounds stressful. But cooking will never, ever get easier if you don't do it. Trust me. Eddie and I have this discussion often and it usually occurs after he's tried to make dinner, has used eight different pots and pans, and still doesn't have the outcome he desired. He always has one thing though: a giant mess!

Here are my top tips if you want to learn how to cook without a recipe! It's really a wonderful thing to do, because you can look at a recipe for guidance and ideas instead of using it as a strict roadmap.

Learn your spice cabinet.

So much of cooking without a recipe comes down to spices and seasonings. It's where people get super freaked out—I mean, how do you know how much garlic powder to add? How much is too much cayenne?

Once you're familiar with spices and know the basics—garlic and onion powders, spices that add smokiness, ones that add spice, and what to do with dried herbs—you have a wealth of knowledge in your hands. It's half the battle.

I've always gone by the rule of starting with ½ teaspoon of most spices, with the exception of spicy ones. Now, there are many dishes where ½ teaspoon doesn't even register, so of course I add a lot more. But once you learn your spices and taste as you go, you will have an idea of how much you need to use.

Learn the basics.

There are a few things that everyone should know how to do: Cooking pasta and grains, scrambling or frying an egg, roasting vegetables, making a quick pan sauce, and seasoning a salad are at the top of my list.

Let go of perfectionism.

While I occasionally like to bake, *cooking* is where my passion lies. Because, honestly? I hate to be told what to do. Yes, this sounds like a personal problem, but the truth is that I want to be in control and I definitely don't want to follow the rules.

Cooking allows a little room for error; you don't need to be so precise. If not following an exact formula stresses you out, start with a dish that you know well. Something as easy as scrambled eggs. You probably don't measure out the salt and the pepper, right?

And with that being said . . .

You can always add more.

Whenever you're adding ingredients, start with less. You can ALWAYS add more, but it is nearly impossible to remove ingredients once added. I'd love to tell that to my twenty-year-old self when I made chili and accidentally added in three full tablespoons of salt. When you add too much of something, you either lose the whole dish or have to overcompensate with more of everything else.

By starting small and adding in, say, ¼ or ½ teaspoon of spice, or maybe 1 to 2 tablespoons of liquid, you can always add more. Of course, this differs per recipe, but the general rule still stands. START WITH LESS.

Taste as you go.

I'm a broken record, yes. But this is key. When I started tasting my food as I cooked, it was a HUGE game changer. Honestly, it's probably the number one thing that helped me learn how to cook without a recipe.

Here's the kicker: Once you taste as you go, you not only learn what you like, but you also end up stamping the amounts into your brain. You learn that you like five cracks of fresh pepper in your soup and one tablespoon of cumin in your tacos instead of two because you do it over and over again. This is why it's important to cook often. It becomes ingrained in your head and soon enough, you will learn how much to add.

Build flavor from the bottom up.

This is one of the most important things I do in my kitchen and why so many of my dishes turn out delicious.

Whether it's a soup, burger, salad, or pot roast, I always start with flavor at the beginning of the recipe. This includes a fat like olive oil or butter, often an onion and garlic, and spices and seasonings. I call them the building blocks of flavor.

This allows the flavor to develop from the start of the recipe and it changes everything—especially when it comes to quick recipes that you can make in 30 minutes! Don't wait until the end to add in a teaspoon of salt. Season your ingredients at the base and taste as you go from there.

Make what you love.

Especially when starting out, consider the flavors that you enjoy. Take your favorite pasta dish and use the flavors in that to create a pizza or taco or burger or salad. Let your favorite flavors inspire you to try new dishes.

Master your technique.

This is something else that ONLY comes when you cook often: your own technique. It's the reason people have a secret chocolate chip cookie recipe or make the best chicken pot pie. My grandma didn't measure a thing but her technique was spot-on, resulting in perfect pie crust every time. No recipe to be found!

When you cook often, you develop a technique that will spill over into all the recipes you try, allowing you to become more comfortable and confident.

Be open-minded.

I can't stand fennel seeds so I'm almost never going to cook with them. But guess what? I also thought that I didn't like rosemary, and then I started adding it to a handful of recipes and it made a huge difference. Sometimes certain ingredients enhance a dish and take on a different flavor.

HOW I LEARNED TO LOVE VEGETABLES, AND STEPS I TAKE TO MAKE SURE MY KIDS DO, TOO!

Sometimes it still shocks me to a level ten: I enjoy eating vegetables every single day. This is HUGE, guys. Huge, I tell you. I spent all of my childhood and, honestly, a good portion of my adult life absolutely loathing vegetables.

Never choosing them if they were in front of me. Not even wanting to eat them as a side dish. Refusing to try them prepared in a different way. I mean, it was so bad that I didn't even like the fact that most soups started with sautéed vegetables, and I certainly wouldn't eat any of the carrots or celery in chicken pot pie.

It was no one's fault, really. Except for my own. My mom cooked incredible dinners every single night of the week, and they usually included vegetables. I just never took to them.

These days, I'm asked all the time how I ended up enjoying vegetable dishes and even sometimes craving them. I have to tell you—it wasn't doing one of these things below that changed my vegetable-hating ways. It was consistency. It was also the realization that I had to parent myself (Mel Robbins coming in hot here). I set a goal to eat some sort of vegetable every single day, which was, of course, easier once my kids came along—I wanted to set a good example. Here are a few of my love-your-vegetable hacks.

PREP THEM IN ADVANCE. This is a big one. Wash and chop any and all vegetables that come into your house immediately. This can be for raw consumption, but, honestly, I usually prep them to roast. I chop broccoli, cauliflower, kale, and more, then place them in a container or resealable bag with a paper towel.

ROAST THE HECK OUT OF THEM. Roasting them brings such a sweet, caramelly yet savory flavor. I find that roasting almost any vegetable at 425°F for 15 to 20 minutes greatly improves the flavor.

ADD OTHER INGREDIENTS YOU REALLY LOVE. Yes, this means cheese! For me, the secret was (and is) Parmesan. I also often add toasted pine nuts or walnuts for crunch. And, of course, I serve some veggies to my kids that have a blanket of fresh melted Cheddar on top.

MAKE RAINBOW MEALS. This one may apply more to children, but if you're a '90s-era Lisa Frank sticker–loving soul like myself, who craves bright colors and rainbows, plating some vegetables in ROYGBIV form may be the game changer.

MAKE A KILLER DIP. While I still prefer my vegetables roasted over raw, if I make a delicious dip, I'll eat them in any form. This includes hummus, pestos, guacamoles, cheese dips, and yogurt dips. You can find lots of them in the sauces section.

MAKE SLAWS FOR TOPPING. Coleslaw never interested me because I don't like creamy dressings, but years ago I started making my own slaws with vinegar-based dressings. They add crunch and texture to sandwiches or meats and are something I really look forward to. They actually made me fall in love with all kinds of cabbage.

MIX THEM INTO SAUCES, CURRIES, AND SOUPS. Seems like a no-brainer, but if you throw some vegetables into a sauce or soup, they are a million times easier to consume.

SEASON SALADS. I never wanted to eat salads growing up unless it was in a restaurant. And I eventually figured out that seasoning was the key. Season your greens with salt and pepper generously, right before assembling the salad. This adds more flavor than you can imagine and is a huge reason that salads in restaurants taste so good. Don't skip this!

ADD SPINACH AND CAULIFLOWER TO SMOOTHIES. These are the two least offensive vegetables in smoothies, which is why I mention them. I started doing this over a decade ago and while it certainly hides the vegetables (which isn't my favorite method of consumption), it's a great way to sneak them in.

SERVE THEM OFTEN, AS IN EVERY DAY. There is no way around this one. The more you eat vegetables, the more you will crave them!

WHAT TO KEEP IN YOUR PANTRY FOR EASY WEEKNIGHT MEALS

- Kosher salt and black pepper
- Flaked sea salt
- Spices and dried herbs: garlic powder, smoked paprika, cumin, chili powder, basil, oregano, and crushed red pepper flakes
- Vinegars: apple cider, red wine, and champagne
- Beans: chickpeas, black beans, and cannellini beans
- Pasta: short cut and long noodles
- Grains: rice, quinoa, couscous, and farro
- Condiments: Dijon, yellow, and grainy mustards; mayonnaise
- Oils: extra-virgin olive, avocado, coconut, canola, and toasted sesame
- Olive oil and high-heat oil sprays
- Nuts: sliced almonds, pine nuts, walnuts, pistachios, and cashews
- Bread crumbs: panko and fine (I like using seasoned varieties)
- Canned tomatoes: crushed, fire roasted, jarred marinara sauce, and tomato paste
- Stock and broth: chicken, vegetable, and beef
- Wine: dry whites and full-bodied reds
- Sugars and sweeteners: brown sugar, granulated sugar, honey, and maple syrup
- Sauces: Worcestershire, Thai sweet chili, and soy
- Anchovy paste
- All-purpose flour
- Tuna packed in olive oil

FIVE THINGS I LIKE TO PREP AT THE BEGINNING OF THE WEEK TO MAKE DINNER EASIER AND THEY BARELY TAKE ANY TIME AT ALL.

FRIDGE ESSENTIALS

You'll find these recipes in the coming pages because I love to make a few simple things to keep in my fridge that help elevate everyday meals. I'm talking about things like pesto, pickled onions, homemade vinaigrette, and salsa. They take only ten minutes to prepare but can bring life to many recipes.

EGGS

I always, always hard-boil a few eggs at the beginning of the week. We often use these on salads or even chopped over roasted asparagus. Don't underestimate the egg! By having a few prepped, you can make a quick garden salad into a heartier and more satisfying meal for dinner. And if we don't eat them for dinner, I can always find a use for them for lunch or breakfast.

To make the perfect hard-boiled eggs, place them in a pot and cover with cold water. Bring the water to a boil over medium heat and let it boil for ONE minute only. Turn off the heat, cover the pot, and let it sit for 10 minutes. After 10 minutes, dunk the eggs in an ice bath and let them cool down.

GRAINS AND/OR POTATOES

I like to prep at least one grain (my favorites are quinoa and farro) to store in the fridge for dinners. Some grains take 30 minutes to cook, but that time is hands-off. Rinsing and measuring the grain takes less than 2 minutes! I usually prep 1 to 2 cups of grains for our family, but if I have a specific recipe in mind for later in the week, I may prep more. Leftover grains make great breakfast bowls, too.

When it comes to potatoes, parboiling them for 5 minutes makes life so much easier. Parboiling basically means to partially cook the potatoes by boiling them for a few minutes. I use the parboiled potatoes as a base for smashed potatoes or I toss them in a skillet to make breakfast for dinner. You can also chop and roast them for a shorter time than if the potatoes were raw.

BEANS

Whether you used canned beans (I do!) or soak your own, having them prepped for the week makes it easier to throw a meal together. I will drain and rinse cans of beans and then store them in the fridge. Sometimes I'll marinate beans for salads or roast chickpeas for snacking. My favorites are chickpeas and cannellini beans. Black beans are a great option, too!

VEGETABLES

I always, always wash and chop cruciferous vegetables (including broccoli, cauliflower, Brussels sprouts, and kale) so they are ready to go for the week. When it comes to greens, I sometimes wash and dry them and then store them in a glass container layered with paper towels until ready to use.

SAUCES, DRESSINGS,

and my favorite recipes
to keep in the fridge

This may be my favorite chapter in the entire book. And there's a good reason for that. Sauces, dressings, and recipes that I make to keep in my fridge can elevate ANY meal. They take "regular" everyday meals over the top, make salads and chicken taste extra delicious, and give all sorts of dishes an extra pop. By adding some pickled onions to the top of a sandwich or drizzling an incredible vinaigrette on top of a house salad, my dishes taste restaurant-ish and it's one of my best secrets.

A few years ago, my friend—the fabulous writer Rachel Wilkerson Miller—dubbed something similar to this the "sauce theory." The premise is that making one or two sauces a week and storing them in the fridge allows variety to creep into everyday meals while also preventing the waste of time, food, and ingredients. I absolutely love this!

In this section you'll find a ton of my favorite dressings, the garlic confit that has changed our life (page 36), a quick guac (page 39), and pico de gallo (page 39) along with delicious sauces like cremas and Peach BBQ sauce (page 47). Most of these recipes play into the 10-Minute Meal Prep rule and will be a game changer for your daily meals.

QUICK PICKLED ONIONS

MAKES 1½ CUPS

1 red onion, thinly sliced

½ cup warm water

1½ tablespoons sugar

1 teaspoon coarse salt

¾ cup apple cider vinegar

Place the onion in a large jar or cup. In a small bowl, whisk together the warm water, sugar, and salt until the sugar and salt dissolve. Whisk in the vinegar. Pour the vinegar mixture over the sliced onion. Let it sit at room temperature, loosely covered, for 30 minutes to 1 hour.

You can make this ahead of time and store it for up to a week in the fridge in a sealed container or jar.

QUICK PICKLED RED CABBAGE

MAKES 1½ CUPS

1 small head of red cabbage, chopped or shredded into thin pieces (about 1½ cups)

½ cup warm water

1½ tablespoons sugar

1 teaspoon coarse salt

¾ cup apple cider vinegar

Place the cabbage in a large jar or bowl. In a smaller bowl, whisk together the warm water with the sugar and salt until they dissolve. Whisk in the vinegar. Pour the vinegar mixture over the cabbage. Let it sit at room temperature for 30 minutes to 1 hour. If making it ahead of time, you can stick it directly in the fridge.

WEEKLY TOMATO CONFIT, TWO WAYS

MAKES 1½ CUPS

STOVETOP

3 cups cherry tomatoes, stems removed

1 cup extra-virgin olive oil

2 sprigs of fresh thyme

4 garlic cloves

In a saucepan, combine the tomatoes, olive oil, thyme sprigs, and garlic. Cook over low heat, barely simmering, until the tomatoes are soft and almost bursting, about 45 minutes. Let cool completely. Store the tomato mixture in a sealed container in the fridge for up to 1 week.

OVEN

3 cups cherry tomatoes, stems removed

1 cup extra-virgin olive oil

½ teaspoon dried thyme

4 garlic cloves

Preheat the oven to 275°F.

In a baking dish, gently toss the tomatoes, olive oil, thyme, and garlic. Roast for 1 hour, until the tomatoes are soft and almost bursting. Let cool completely. Store the tomato mixture in a sealed container in the fridge for up to 1 week.

WEEKLY GARLIC CONFIT, TWO WAYS

MAKES 1 CUP

1 cup extra-virgin olive oil

1 cup whole, peeled garlic cloves (about 3 heads of garlic)

A few sprigs of fresh thyme

Stovetop method: Combine the olive oil, garlic, and thyme in a saucepan over low heat. Cook for 30 to 45 minutes, until the cloves are caramel in color. Let the mixture cool completely. Pour into a jar and store in the fridge, covered, up to 1 week.

Roast method: Preheat the oven to 225°F. Place the olive oil, garlic, and thyme in a baking dish. Bake for 2 hours. Let cool completely. Pour into a jar and store in the fridge, covered, up to 1 week.

APPLE CIDER CARAMELIZED ONIONS

MAKES ½ CUP

4 tablespoons unsalted butter

2 large sweet onions, thinly sliced

½ teaspoon kosher salt

4 tablespoons apple cider

Heat a heavy-bottomed saucepan over medium-low heat and add the butter. Once melted, stir in the onions and salt. Stir and cook for 5 minutes, until the onions begin to soften.

Reduce the heat to low. Add in a tablespoon of the apple cider. Cook, stirring often, for 30 minutes, adding 1 tablespoon of apple cider every 10 minutes. This prevents the onions from drying out and also lets them slowly caramelize with the cider.

Be sure to keep the onions over low heat so they don't burn. Once they are done, use them or store them in a sealed container in the fridge for up to 3 days.

TACO SAUCE

MAKES 1½ CUPS

1 cup canned tomato sauce

1½ teaspoons ground cumin

1 teaspoon smoked paprika

1 teaspoon onion powder

1 teaspoon garlic powder

½ teaspoon chili powder

½ teaspoon kosher salt

¼ teaspoon freshly ground black pepper

Pinch of crushed red pepper flakes

1 tablespoon apple cider vinegar

1 teaspoon honey

In a saucepan, combine the tomato sauce, ½ cup water, cumin, smoked paprika, onion powder, garlic powder, chili powder, salt, black pepper, red pepper flakes, vinegar, and honey. Bring to a simmer over medium heat and let simmer for 5 minutes. Let the mixture cool completely.

Carefully transfer the mixture to a blender and blend until smooth. Keep stored in the fridge for up to 2 weeks.

QUICK PICO DE GALLO

MAKES 1½ CUPS

1 pint cherry tomatoes, quartered

½ sweet onion, diced

¼ cup fresh cilantro, chopped

Juice of half a lime

Pinch of kosher salt and black pepper

In a bowl, toss together the tomatoes, onion, cilantro, and lime juice. Season with the salt and pepper. This stays great in the fridge for up to 3 days.

QUICK AND EASY GUACAMOLE

MAKES ABOUT 1 CUP

2 medium avocados

½ jalapeño pepper, seeded and diced

¼ sweet onion, diced

3 tablespoons chopped fresh cilantro

Juice of 1 lime, plus additional if needed

Kosher salt and black pepper

In a medium bowl, mash the avocados. Stir in the jalapeño, onion, cilantro, and lime juice. Add ½ teaspoon each of salt and pepper and mash again. Taste and season with additional salt, pepper, and lime juice if needed.

TAHINI SAUCE

MAKES 1½ CUPS

½ cup tahini

½ cup warm water

1 tablespoon lime juice

1 garlic clove

¼ to ½ teaspoon kosher salt

¼ teaspoon freshly ground black pepper

Scant ¼ teaspoon smoked paprika

In a food processor or blender, combine the tahini, warm water, lime juice, garlic, salt, pepper, and smoked paprika. Process until smooth and combined, scraping down the sides when needed. Store the sauce in a sealed container in the fridge for up to 5 days.

Roasted Sweet Potatoes with Honey Ginger Chickpeas   95

Roasted Kabocha Squash Grain Bowls   100

FIRE ROASTED MARINARA

MAKES ABOUT 3 CUPS

2 (14-ounce) cans fire roasted diced tomatoes

2 garlic cloves, minced

1 shallot, diced

½ cup fresh basil, torn or chopped

½ teaspoon dried basil

3 tablespoons unsalted butter

1 teaspoon brown sugar

½ teaspoon kosher salt

Pinch of freshly cracked black pepper

In a saucepan, combine the tomatoes, garlic, shallot, fresh and dried basil, butter, brown sugar, salt, and pepper over medium heat. Once simmering, cover and cook for 30 minutes, stirring occasionally. As the tomatoes get softer, mash them to your preferred texture with a fork or the back of a spoon.

After 30 minutes, you can use the sauce as is, if you like it a little chunky, or you can transfer it to a blender and puree until smooth. Store in the fridge for up to 1 week.

PESTO, TWO WAYS

MAKES ABOUT 1 CUP

CLASSIC PESTO

¼ cup pine nuts

4 cups loosely packed fresh basil leaves

½ cup finely grated Parmesan cheese

3 garlic cloves

½ to ¾ cup extra-virgin olive oil

¼ teaspoon kosher salt

¼ teaspoon black pepper

¼ teaspoon crushed red pepper flakes

Toast the pine nuts: In a small dry skillet, toast the pine nuts over low heat. Shake and stir until the nuts are golden and fragrant, about 5 minutes. Remove from the heat and set aside to cool.

In a food processor, combine the basil, Parmesan, pine nuts, and garlic. Pulse until finely chopped, and then—with the processor running—stream in the olive oil. Start with ½ cup and add the extra if needed to reach the desired consistency. Add the salt, black pepper, and red pepper flakes and blend again. Taste and season if needed. This stays great in the fridge for a week or the freezer for 3 months.

VARIATION

Swap the basil out for baby arugula or spinach.

PISTACHIO PESTO

1½ cups loosely packed fresh basil leaves, torn

1 cup shelled pistachios

½ cup baby spinach or arugula

3 garlic cloves

½ to ¾ cup extra-virgin olive oil

¼ teaspoon kosher salt

¼ teaspoon black pepper

¼ teaspoon crushed red pepper flakes

In a food processor, combine the basil, pistachios, spinach, and garlic. Pulse until finely chopped, and then—with the processor running—stream in the olive oil. Start with ½ cup and add the extra if needed to reach the desired consistency. Add the salt, black pepper, and red pepper flakes and blend again. Taste and season if needed. This stays great in the fridge for a week or the freezer for 3 months.

ROASTED RED PEPPER SAUCE, TWO WAYS

MAKES ABOUT 2 CUPS

SEMI-HOMEMADE

2 (16-ounce) jars roasted red peppers, plus ¼ cup liquid from the jar

⅓ cup finely grated Parmesan cheese

4 to 5 fresh basil leaves, torn

¼ teaspoon black pepper

⅛ teaspoon kosher salt

In a blender, combine the jarred peppers and the ¼ cup of liquid, the Parmesan, basil, black pepper, and salt. Puree until smooth. Note: depending on the brand of jarred peppers you use, your sauce may be slightly sweeter than expected. Don't be afraid to add another pinch of salt to balance it out.

FROM SCRATCH

2 large red bell peppers

1 garlic clove

⅓ cup finely grated Parmesan cheese

4 to 5 fresh basil leaves, torn

¼ teaspoon black pepper

⅛ teaspoon kosher salt

3 to 4 tablespoons extra-virgin olive oil

To roast the peppers: Preheat the broiler. Remove the core and seeds from the peppers and slice the peppers into pieces. Place them on a baking sheet and broil skin side up until the skins are completely charred and black. This took about 10 minutes for me but the timing will depend on your oven; just check every 2 minutes or so. Immediately remove the peppers from oven and, using kitchen tongs, quickly place them in a resealable bag. Seal the bag and set aside for 20 to 30 minutes.

To make the sauce, remove the peppers from the bag and peel off and discard the skins. It's okay if a little bit of char remains as it adds to the flavor. In a food processor, combine the peppers, garlic, Parmesan, basil, black pepper, and salt. Blend until pureed. With the food processor running, stream in the olive oil so the mixture comes together.

Store in a sealed container in the fridge for up to 5 days.

GREEN GODDESS SAUCE

MAKES 1½ CUPS

1 medium avocado

⅔ cup plain Greek yogurt
(I like full fat or 2%)

⅓ cup mayonnaise

2 garlic cloves

¼ cup chopped fresh parsley

¼ cup chopped fresh basil leaves

2 tablespoons snipped fresh
chives

Juice of half a lemon

Kosher salt and black pepper
to taste

In a food processor, combine the avocado, yogurt, mayonnaise, garlic, parsley, basil, chives, lemon juice, and salt and pepper. Blend until combined.

Keep in a sealed container in the fridge for up to 5 days.

CHIPOTLE CREMA

MAKES ¾ CUP

2 tablespoons sour cream

¾ cup half-and-half

1 tablespoon adobo sauce (from
a can of chipotles in adobo)

Juice of half a lime

⅛ teaspoon kosher salt

In a blender or food processor, combine the sour cream, half-and-half, adobo sauce, lime juice, and salt. Blend until smooth.

Keep in a sealed container in the fridge for 3 to 4 days.

PEACH BBQ SAUCE

MAKES ABOUT 1 CUP

2 cups peeled and chopped fresh peaches (about 2 large peaches)

¼ cup ketchup

⅔ cup water or beer (I prefer a light wheat or amber ale for this recipe)

¼ cup honey

3 garlic cloves, minced

2 tablespoons apple cider vinegar

2 tablespoons Dijon mustard

1 teaspoon Worcestershire sauce

½ teaspoon onion powder

½ teaspoon smoked paprika

¼ teaspoon freshly ground black pepper

In a saucepan over medium heat, combine the chopped peaches, ketchup, water or beer, honey, garlic, vinegar, mustard, Worcestershire sauce, onion powder, smoked paprika, and pepper. Cook, stirring often, for 20 minutes or until the peaches begin to soften. Cover and cook for 20 to 30 minutes more, continuing to stir as it cooks.

Carefully transfer the sauce to a blender or food processor. Puree until smooth. Let the mixture come to room temperature so it thickens. Refrigerate. This sauce stays great for about a week in the fridge.

AVOCADO CREMA

MAKES ½ CUP

⅓ cup plain Greek yogurt or sour cream

1 medium avocado

Juice of 1 to 2 limes

Pinch of kosher salt and black pepper

In a food processor or blender, combine the yogurt, avocado, juice of 1 lime, salt, and pepper. Blend until smooth. If you'd like more liquid, add the juice of the second lime. Use leftovers as a dip. Stores well in the fridge for 2 to 3 days.

AVOCADO BUTTERMILK DRESSING AND DIP

MAKES ¾ CUP

1 medium avocado

½ cup buttermilk (recipe follows)

2 tablespoons mayonnaise

1 tablespoon chopped fresh chives

1 teaspoon chopped fresh parsley

1 teaspoon chopped fresh dill

1 garlic clove, minced

¼ teaspoon white vinegar

⅛ teaspoon kosher salt

⅛ teaspoon black pepper

3 tablespoons extra-virgin olive oil

In a food processor, combine the avocado, buttermilk, mayonnaise, chives, parsley, dill, garlic, vinegar, salt, pepper, and olive oil. Blend until smooth.

Keep in a sealed container in the fridge for 3 to 4 days.

how to make your own buttermilk

MAKES 1 CUP

1 cup milk (whole, 2%, or skim is fine)

1 teaspoon lemon juice or vinegar

In a measuring cup or bowl, whisk together the milk and lemon juice and let sit at room temperature for 10 minutes before using.

AVOCADO HERB SAUCE

MAKES ½ CUP

1 avocado

Grated zest and juice of 1 lime

½ cup fresh herbs, like a mix of basil and cilantro

¼ cup extra-virgin olive oil

In a food processor, combine the avocado, lime zest and juice, and the herbs. Blend until combined. With the food processor on, stream in the olive oil and blend until creamy and smooth. This stays great in the fridge for 1 to 2 days.

STRAWBERRY–BLACK PEPPER BUTTERMILK DRESSING

MAKES ½ CUP

8 large strawberries, hulled and sliced

¼ cup buttermilk (page 48)

2 tablespoons chopped fresh chives

2 tablespoons plain Greek yogurt

2 tablespoons extra-virgin olive oil

1 tablespoon red or white wine vinegar

1 teaspoon freshly ground black pepper

½ teaspoon kosher salt

In a blender or food processor, combine the strawberries, buttermilk, chives, yogurt, olive oil, vinegar, pepper, and salt. Blend until smooth and creamy. This stays great in the fridge for 2 to 3 days.

BLUE CHEESE VINAIGRETTE

MAKES ⅔ CUP

3 tablespoons white wine vinegar

1 garlic clove, minced

1 tablespoon chopped fresh chives

1 tablespoon chopped fresh dill

1 tablespoon honey

1 teaspoon Dijon mustard

Pinch of kosher salt and black pepper

½ cup extra-virgin olive oil

3 tablespoons crumbled blue cheese

In a small bowl, whisk together the vinegar, garlic, chives, dill, honey, mustard, salt, and pepper. Stream in the olive oil while whisking until emulsified. Stir in the blue cheese. This stays great in the fridge for 2 to 3 days.

CHILI-LIME VINAIGRETTE

MAKES ⅔ CUP

1 tablespoon red wine vinegar

1 garlic clove, minced

Grated zest and juice of 1 lime

1½ tablespoons honey

2 teaspoons chili oil

Pinch of kosher salt and black pepper

½ cup extra-virgin olive oil

In a small bowl, whisk together the vinegar, garlic, lime zest and juice, honey, chili oil, salt, pepper, and olive oil until combined. Drizzle over salad. Dressing stays great in the fridge for 3 to 4 days.

BALSAMIC VINAIGRETTE

MAKES ⅔ CUP

2 tablespoons balsamic vinegar

1 garlic clove, minced

1 teaspoon brown sugar

½ teaspoon Dijon mustard

Pinch of kosher salt and black pepper

½ cup extra-virgin olive oil

In a small bowl, whisk together the vinegar, garlic, brown sugar, mustard, salt, and pepper. Stream in the olive oil while whisking until the dressing is emulsified. Store in a sealed container in the fridge and shake or whisk before using.

BASIL VINAIGRETTE

MAKES ⅔ CUP

1 cup tightly packed fresh basil leaves

1 garlic clove, minced

1 tablespoon lemon juice

½ tablespoon apple cider vinegar

½ teaspoon kosher salt

½ teaspoon black pepper

⅓ cup extra-virgin olive oil

In a blender or food processor, combine the basil, garlic, lemon juice, vinegar, salt, pepper, and olive oil. Blend until smooth. Store this in a sealed container in the fridge for 3 to 4 days.

OUR FAVORITE RANCH

MAKES 2½ CUPS

1 cup plain Greek yogurt

½ cup mayonnaise

½ cup milk

3 tablespoons fresh chives
or 1 tablespoon dried chives

2 tablespoons fresh dill or
2 teaspoons dried dill weed

1 tablespoon fresh parsley
or 1 teaspoon dried parsley

2 teaspoons freshly squeezed
lemon juice

1 teaspoon garlic powder

½ teaspoon onion powder

½ teaspoon kosher salt

½ teaspoon freshly ground black
pepper

¼ teaspoon smoked paprika

In a food processor or blender, combine the yogurt, mayonnaise, milk, chives, dill, parsley, lemon juice, garlic powder, onion powder, salt, pepper, and smoked paprika. Blend until smooth. This stays great in the fridge for 1 week. It can be used as a dressing or a dip!

CAESAR YOGURT DRESSING

MAKES ⅔ CUP

2 garlic cloves, minced

3 tablespoons plain Greek yogurt

2 tablespoons grated Parmesan cheese

1 tablespoon Dijon mustard

2 teaspoons red wine vinegar

1 teaspoon anchovy paste

Juice of half a lemon

¼ teaspoon kosher salt

¼ teaspoon black pepper

½ cup extra-virgin olive oil

In a food processor, combine the garlic, yogurt, Parmesan, mustard, vinegar, anchovy paste, lemon juice, salt, and pepper. Blend until pureed. With the processor still on, stream in the olive oil until a creamy dressing forms. Store in a sealed container in the fridge for up to 5 days and stir well before using.

CINNAMON SHALLOT VINAIGRETTE

MAKES ½ CUP

2 tablespoons red wine vinegar

1½ tablespoons honey

1 teaspoon Dijon mustard

1 shallot, diced

1 garlic clove, minced

¼ to ½ teaspoon ground cinnamon

¼ teaspoon kosher salt

¼ teaspoon black pepper

⅓ cup extra-virgin olive oil

In a small bowl, whisk together the vinegar, honey, mustard, shallot, garlic, cinnamon, salt, and pepper. Whisk in the olive oil until emulsified. This keeps great in the fridge for 3 to 4 days.

JAM VINAIGRETTE

MAKES ¾ CUP

¼ cup apple cider vinegar

2 tablespoons jam (I like apricot, strawberry, fig, and orange marmalade)

2 garlic cloves, finely minced or pressed

Pinch of kosher salt and black pepper

Pinch of crushed red pepper flakes

½ cup extra-virgin olive oil

In a small bowl, whisk together the vinegar, jam, garlic, salt, black pepper, and red pepper flakes. Continue to whisk while streaming in the olive oil. This dressing stays great in the fridge in a sealed container for a week or so, so feel free to make a double batch if desired!

HONEY MUSTARD VINAIGRETTE

MAKES ⅔ CUP

3 tablespoons apple cider vinegar

2 tablespoons honey

1 tablespoon Dijon mustard

2 garlic cloves, finely minced or pressed

Pinch of kosher salt and black pepper

½ cup extra-virgin olive oil

In a small bowl, whisk together the vinegar, honey, mustard, garlic, salt, and pepper. Continue to whisk while streaming in the olive oil. This dressing stays great in the fridge in a sealed container for a week or so.

CITRUS VINAIGRETTE

MAKES ½ CUP

2 tablespoons diced shallot

2 tablespoons freshly squeezed lime juice

1 teaspoon freshly grated orange zest

1 tablespoon freshly squeezed orange juice

½ teaspoon honey

Pinch of kosher salt and black pepper

½ cup extra-virgin olive oil

In a small bowl, whisk together the shallot, lime juice, orange zest, orange juice, honey, salt, and pepper. Whisk in the olive oil until the dressing is emulsified. This dressing stays great in the fridge for 3 to 4 days.

HOUSE VINAIGRETTE

MAKES ⅔ CUP

3 tablespoons freshly squeezed lemon juice

1 tablespoon red wine vinegar

2 teaspoons honey

½ teaspoon Dijon mustard

2 garlic cloves, finely minced or pressed

1 tablespoon finely grated Parmesan cheese

Pinch of kosher salt and black pepper

Pinch of crushed red pepper flakes

½ cup extra-virgin olive oil

In a small bowl, whisk together the lemon juice, vinegar, honey, mustard, garlic, Parmesan, salt, black pepper, and red pepper flakes. Continue to whisk while streaming in the olive oil. This dressing stays great sealed in the fridge for 3 to 4 days.

MEATLESS MEALS

(everything from salad to
pasta to breakfast for dinner.
and, yes, there is cheese!)

Even though my husband is a proud carnivore, meatless meals are where I shine for dinner. They are what I love to eat, where I find the most creativity, and what I love to serve friends and family. Of course, I still allow copious amounts of cheese and I often throw an egg on top, but still. These meals are a delight.

In this section you'll find a plethora of salads, soups, grain bowls, sandwiches, pastas, and pizzas. They are filling enough if you enjoy eating a meatless meal but many of them allow for the addition of your favorite meat, chicken, or shrimp. Lots of these work great as leftovers and many of them can be prepped ahead of time.

HARVEST HONEYCRISP SALAD

SERVES 2 TO 4 | TIME: 25 MINUTES

This salad is the epitome of fall. It's spiced and flavorful and crunchy, highlighting juicy Honeycrisp apples (the absolute best!) and drizzled all over with a cinnamon vinaigrette. Toasted almonds give it fabulous texture, too.

This is a salad that works for a family dinner, but it's also a wonderful addition to a dinner party or potluck. Kale holds up so well that the salad doesn't wilt in transport. It's a simple but delicious bowl of greens!

6 cups chopped Tuscan kale

Cinnamon Shallot Vinaigrette (page 55)

Kosher salt and black pepper to taste

⅓ cup sliced almonds

2 Honeycrisp apples, thinly sliced

2 tablespoons roasted, salted pepitas

3 ounces freshly grated sharp white Cheddar cheese

In a large bowl, massage the kale with a tablespoon or so of the vinaigrette and let it sit for 5 to 10 minutes. Season the kale with salt and pepper.

While the kale is marinating, heat a skillet over medium-low heat and add the almonds. Cook, stirring often, until the almonds are golden and fragrant, about 6 to 8 minutes. Don't take your eyes off them as they can burn easily.

Combine the sliced apples and almonds with the kale and toss well. Top with the pepitas and Cheddar. Serve with more vinaigrette!

10-MINUTE MEAL PREP

● The almonds can be toasted ahead of time and stored in the fridge or pantry for 24 hours.

STONE FRUIT HALLOUMI SALAD

SERVES 4 | TIME: 25 MINUTES

Halloumi has been a life-changing discovery for me in the last decade. This savory cheese takes on a new life when seared in a skillet, revealing crispy golden bits on the outside that make your mouth water. It is divine! It also adds a nice heartiness to whatever meal it's added to.

Ripe, juicy fruits; peppery arugula; and creamy, salty halloumi cheese all drizzled with a basil vinaigrette: It's everything I want on a plate come July and August. Plus, it's super pretty!

8 ounces halloumi cheese, sliced into ½-inch pieces

1 tablespoon extra-virgin olive oil

6 to 8 cups baby arugula

Kosher salt and black pepper

2 peaches, pitted and sliced

2 plums, pitted and sliced

2 pluots, pitted and sliced

1 cup cherries, pitted and sliced

Basil Vinaigrette (page 52)

3 tablespoons chopped fresh herbs, like basil or parsley

To crisp the halloumi, heat a nonstick skillet over medium-high heat. Pat the halloumi dry with a paper towel. Add the olive oil to the skillet. Add the halloumi and cook until golden brown on each side, about 2 to 3 minutes per side. Remove the halloumi and place it on a plate. If you want the halloumi to be warm when serving, you can assemble the salad first!

Place the arugula on a large plate. Season with a pinch of salt and pepper. Top with the sliced peaches, plums, pluots, and cherries. Add on the crisp halloumi. Drizzle everything with the basil vinaigrette and a sprinkling of fresh herbs. Serve immediately.

10-MINUTE MEAL PREP

- The basil vinaigrette can be made ahead of time.

- The cherries can be pitted and sliced ahead of time, though I prefer to slice the peaches, plums, and pluots right before serving.

BRUSSELS AND KALE CAESAR
with buffalo chickpeas

SERVES 2 AS A MEAL, 4 AS A SIDE DISH | TIME: 30 MINUTES

You're probably realizing by now that I really love kale salads. It's actually mind-blowing to me, too—after years of avoiding vegetables, my favorites have become the ones that most people avoid: Brussels sprouts and kale.

A kale Caesar salad is one of our staple weeknight meals, and there's one reason: It's super hearty. Kale salad lasts and gets even better as it sits; the leaves break down and become deliciously chewy and lose their bitterness. It's also Eddie's favorite salad, so I make it at least once a week.

After falling in love with Caesar salads, I started adding warm shredded Brussels sprouts to the kale, too. The texture is outstanding. The flavor is fabulous.

And because it's so hearty, it can take on almost anything as a topping! My favorite is buffalo fried chickpeas, but pick whatever you love: shrimp, chicken, salmon, even a big pan of roasted vegetables. You can't go wrong.

1 bunch Tuscan kale, leaves torn from stems

1 tablespoon extra-virgin olive oil

1 pound Brussels sprouts, sliced and stems removed

½ teaspoon kosher salt

½ teaspoon freshly cracked black pepper

2 tablespoons unsalted butter

1 garlic clove, minced or pressed

⅓ cup seasoned panko bread crumbs

Caesar Yogurt Dressing (page 55)

1 handful freshly shaved Parmesan cheese

Buffalo Fried Chickpeas (recipe opposite)

Slice the kale into shreds and place it in a large bowl. Set aside.

Heat a skillet over medium-low heat and add the olive oil. Add the Brussels sprouts, salt, and pepper and stir well. Cook the sprouts until warm and slightly soft, about 5 to 6 minutes.

While the sprouts cook, add the butter to a small saucepan over medium heat and whisk constantly while it bubbles. The minute brown bits begin to form on the bottom of the pan, add the minced garlic and bread crumbs. Stirring constantly, cook for 2 to 3 minutes until the bread crumbs are golden and crunchy.

Remove the sprouts from the skillet and place right on top of the kale, while they are still warm. Toss together. This will help the kale begin to wilt. Toss with a few spoonfuls of the Caesar dressing, making sure all of the kale is covered. Let sit for 5 minutes before topping with the garlic bread crumbs, shaved Parmesan, and buffalo fried chickpeas. Drizzle with more dressing if desired.

buffalo fried chickpeas

1 (14-ounce) can chickpeas, drained and rinsed

2 tablespoons extra-virgin olive oil

Pinch of kosher salt and freshly ground black pepper

3 tablespoons buffalo wing sauce, plus more for serving if desired

2 tablespoons chopped fresh chives

1 scallion, thinly sliced

Place the chickpeas on a clean dish towel and gently roll them back and forth to dry them. This will also remove some of the skins, which can be discarded. I don't worry too much about the skins, but I do remove the ones that stand out the most.

Heat a skillet over medium heat and add the olive oil. Add the chickpeas in a single layer (don't overcrowd the skillet—do this in batches if you're making more than 1 can at a time!). Season with the salt and pepper and cook for 5 to 10 minutes, tossing occasionally, until the chickpeas crisp up. Drizzle in the wing sauce and coat, cooking for 2 to 3 more minutes. Transfer the chickpeas to a plate and sprinkle on the chives and scallion. You can drizzle on extra wing sauce if you'd like!

10-MINUTE MEAL PREP

❶ The dressing can be made ahead of time and stored in the fridge.

❷ The bread crumbs can be made ahead of time and stored in a resealable bag in the fridge.

❸ Drain and rinse the chickpeas, then pat dry. Store in a sealed container in the fridge. You may need to pat them dry one more time before using.

AVOCADO-ORANGE SALAD
with 5-minute marcona almond granola

SERVES 4 | TIME: 20 MINUTES

If you haven't tried avocado and citrus fruit together yet, you're in for a treat. The bright, punchy citrus flavors complement the creamy avocado so well. It's a classic combination that I adore, and I love to add extra flavor in the form of citrus vinaigrette made with diced shallots.

The shallots marinate in the dressing and most of the onion "sting" is removed. The icing on the cake is a 5-minute marcona almond granola that you sprinkle on top for crunch. It adds a wonderful texture and the flavor is nutty and savory. You can prep the dressing and granola ahead of time, meaning the salad can come together in about 10 minutes!

Lovely. Just lovely.

4 cups fresh spring greens

Kosher salt and black pepper to taste

2 avocados, thinly sliced

2 blood oranges, peeled and sliced

1 cara cara orange, peeled and sliced

1 grapefruit, peeled and sliced

Citrus Vinaigrette (page 58)

5-Minute Marcona Almond Granola (recipe right)

In a large bowl, toss the greens with salt and pepper. Top with the sliced avocados, blood oranges, cara cara orange, and grapefruit. Drizzle with the vinaigrette and top with the granola.

5-minute marcona almond granola

2 teaspoons extra-virgin olive oil

½ cup marcona almonds, chopped

3 tablespoons chopped walnuts

3 tablespoons old-fashioned oats

1 teaspoon honey

½ teaspoon freshly grated lemon zest

¼ teaspoon smoked paprika

¼ teaspoon kosher salt

¼ teaspoon freshly cracked black pepper

¼ teaspoon crushed red pepper flakes

Heat the olive oil in a skillet over medium heat. Add the almonds, walnuts, and oats and toss. Cook, stirring often, for 2 to 3 minutes or until it all begins to toast. Drizzle in the honey, then add the lemon zest, smoked paprika, salt, black pepper, and red pepper flakes. Toss and stir until everything comes together. Turn off the heat and spread the granola on parchment until cooled.

10-MINUTE MEAL PREP

- Vinaigrette can be made ahead of time and stored in the fridge.
- Granola can be made ahead of time and stored in the fridge.

STRAWBERRY–BLACK PEPPER BUTTERMILK SPINACH SALAD

SERVES 4 | TIME: 25 MINUTES

The classic strawberry spinach salad makes a big appearance in my house in spring. I actually count down the days until we can pick fresh strawberries—there is nothing better! The strawberries we pick are so sweet that they could be dessert all by themselves, and I'm definitely not a person who usually considers fruit to be dessert.

To give this salad a special twist, drizzle on the black pepper buttermilk dressing. It's so creamy and tangy. In fact it's SO good that sometimes I use it as a dip for any fresh fruit.

This salad is crunchy and fresh. You can swap out the greens based on what you have, but the other ingredients are pretty standard: strawberries, avocado, and shallot. It's a tradition here and a great one to bring to a picnic or party.

12 ounces baby spinach

8 ounces strawberries, sliced

2 avocados, thinly sliced

1 shallot, thinly sliced

Pinch of kosher salt and black pepper

Strawberry–Black Pepper Buttermilk Dressing (page 50)

In a large bowl, combine the spinach, strawberries, avocado, and shallot and toss with salt and pepper. Drizzle with the dressing and serve.

10-MINUTE MEAL PREP

- The dressing can be made ahead of time and stored in the fridge for 2 to 3 days.

CAJUN LIME SWEET POTATO SALAD

SERVES 2 TO 4 | TIME: 35 MINUTES

We eat many, many sweet potatoes in this house. They are a definite staple for us, but I'd be lying if I said I didn't get bored of them after a while.

So, enter this Cajun-ish salad bowl! The sweet potatoes are loaded with spices and roasted until soft. Throw them on a bed of greens with feta cheese and avocado and add an addictive chili-lime dressing. The combination is outstanding, and you'll never be bored of sweet potatoes again.

I love to eat this as a delish dinner, but it's perfect as a side dish, too! Pair it with grilled chicken or even steak.

2 medium sweet potatoes, peeled and chopped into 1-inch cubes (about 2 cups)

1 tablespoon extra-virgin olive oil

1 teaspoon smoked paprika

1 teaspoon dried Italian seasoning

1 teaspoon garlic powder

Kosher salt and black pepper

Pinch of cayenne pepper

4 to 6 cups spring greens

1 avocado, cubed

¼ cup crumbled feta cheese

Chili-Lime Vinaigrette (page 51)

Lime wedges, for spritzing

Preheat the oven to 425°F.

Place the sweet potato cubes on a baking sheet. Drizzle with the olive oil and toss. In a small bowl, stir together the smoked paprika, Italian seasoning, garlic powder, and a pinch each of salt, black pepper, and cayenne. Sprinkle the spice mixture over the potatoes and toss to combine. Roast for 20 to 25 minutes, until tender.

While the sweet potatoes roast, place the greens in a bowl with a pinch of salt and pepper. Once the sweet potatoes are done, add them to the greens (they can be warm or cool!), topping with the avocado, feta cheese, and some of the vinaigrette. Serve with lime wedges on the side.

10-MINUTE MEAL PREP

- The sweet potatoes can be peeled, chopped, placed in a bowl of ice water, and stored in the fridge for up to 24 hours. Pat them completely dry before roasting.

- The seasonings can be combined ahead of time and stored in the pantry.

- The vinaigrette can be made ahead of time and stored in the fridge.

HOW SWEET EATS
HOUSE PASTA SALAD

SERVES 4 TO 6 | TIME: 25 MINUTES

I've always loved the idea of having a "signature" thing. By thing, I mean a signature scent, a signature cocktail, a signature *something* that people know they can expect when they come to our home. My mom's signature dish is chicken marsala. When I was a kid, her signature perfume was Dune by Christian Dior. Let's just say she had a lot of signatures.

Enter my house pasta salad. This is a classic—one that can be served for dinner or taken to a potluck. The flavors aren't anything wild, but they work so well together and taste different enough from your traditional pasta salad.

This is one of Eddie's favorite dishes of all time. I surprise him with it as a side dish for some Monday night dinners and it makes an appearance at most cookouts, too. It's a sure winner every time.

1 pound fusilli pasta, cooked

1 (6-ounce) jar sun-dried tomatoes, drained (reserve the oil!) and chopped

1 cup fresh mozzarella balls

3 cups baby spinach or kale

1 tablespoon red wine vinegar

1 teaspoon honey

Pinch of kosher salt and black pepper to taste

1 garlic clove, minced

¼ cup oil from the jar of sun-dried tomatoes (or as much as you can get)

⅓ cup extra-virgin olive oil

In a large bowl, toss together the cooked pasta, sun-dried tomatoes, fresh mozzarella, and spinach.

In a bowl or measuring cup, whisk together the vinegar, honey, salt, pepper, and the garlic. Stream in the sun-dried tomato oil and the olive oil while whisking, until the dressing is somewhat emulsified. Pour over the pasta salad and toss well. This stays great in the fridge for 1 to 2 days.

10-MINUTE MEAL PREP

- The pasta can be cooked ahead of time and stored in the fridge. The tomatoes can be drained and chopped and stored in the fridge.

- The dressing can be made ahead of time.

- The entire salad can be made 24 hours ahead of time, but wait to toss in the spinach until 1 hour before serving.

SUMMER CHICKPEA PASTA SOUP
with rosemary pistou

SERVES 4 TO 6 | TIME: 35 MINUTES

It would be safe to say that pestos and pistous have ruined soup for me, forever. I absolutely crave a drizzle of something extra in my soup these days, especially something as fresh as this rosemary pistou.

A pistou is similar to pesto, but without the nuts. This rosemary version tastes like a bright garden on a perfect summer day! It's delicious in the soup, but also works on things like garlic bread, salads, roasted vegetables, and steak.

Every season is soup season for me, if only because I live for the leftovers. It's also an ideal clean-out-the-fridge meal, which you know by this point, I adore. This recipe uses up some summer vegetables, but is great any time of year!

1 tablespoon extra-virgin olive oil

1 tablespoon unsalted butter

½ cup chopped carrot

½ sweet onion, diced

1 cup diced zucchini

2 garlic cloves, minced

1 tablespoon chopped fresh rosemary

Kosher salt and freshly cracked black pepper

1 (14-ounce) can chickpeas, drained and rinsed

6 cups vegetable stock

1 Parmesan cheese rind

8 ounces short cut pasta, like shells

Freshly grated Parmesan cheese, for serving

Rosemary Pistou (recipe right)

Heat a large pot over medium heat and add the olive oil and butter. Add the carrot, onion, zucchini, garlic, rosemary, and a pinch of salt and pepper. Stir well. Cook for 5 minutes, or until the vegetables soften.

Stir in the chickpeas and vegetable stock. Add the Parmesan rind. Bring the mixture to a simmer.

Add the pasta shells and cook (uncovered) for 10 to 15 minutes, stirring often, until the pasta is al dente. Once finished, taste and season the soup with more salt and pepper if needed. You can remove the Parmesan rind if it hasn't fully dissolved.

Serve immediately with grated Parmesan and the rosemary pistou.

rosemary pistou

2 garlic cloves, minced

1 cup torn fresh basil leaves

2 tablespoons chopped fresh rosemary

Pinch of kosher salt and black pepper

¼ cup extra-virgin olive oil

In a food processor, combine the garlic, basil, rosemary, salt, and pepper and pulse until chopped. Stream in the olive oil with the processor on until just combined. Store in the fridge for 2 to 3 days.

10-MINUTE MEAL PREP

❶ Chop the vegetables ahead of time and store together in the fridge.

❷ Make the pistou up to 24 hours ahead of time and store in the fridge.

BUTTERNUT MINESTRONE

SERVES 6 | TIME: 35 MINUTES

Is there anything more comforting than a bowl of piping hot minestrone, sprinkled with shaved Parmesan? I think not. This bowl is super savory with a hint of sweetness from the squash. It's absolutely LOADED with vegetables.

I love that minestrone is so hearty but made completely of vegetables. I like to bulk mine up with extra spinach, fire roasted tomatoes, and anything else I can find in my fridge that may be on its last leg. You can get away with adding almost anything.

2 tablespoons extra-virgin olive oil

1 sweet onion, diced

2 garlic cloves, minced

Kosher salt and freshly cracked black pepper

¾ cup diced carrots

2 cups cubed butternut squash

1 tablespoon maple syrup

1 Parmesan cheese rind, if you have it

2 (14-ounce) cans cannellini beans, drained and rinsed

2 (14-ounce) cans fire roasted diced tomatoes

6 cups low-sodium vegetable stock

½ teaspoon dried sage

½ teaspoon dried oregano

Pinch of freshly grated nutmeg

1 cup ditalini pasta

6 cups fresh baby spinach

Shaved Parmesan, for topping

Heat a large stock pot over medium-low heat and add the olive oil.

Add in the onion and garlic with 1 teaspoon each of salt and pepper and stir. Cook until the onion is translucent, about 5 to 6 minutes.

Add in the carrots and squash, cooking for 5 minutes more. Drizzle in the maple syrup.

Add in the Parmesan rind (if you're using it), beans, tomatoes, stock, sage, oregano, and nutmeg and stir. Bring the mixture to a boil. Reduce it to a simmer and cook for 15 minutes.

After 15 minutes, add in the ditalini pasta. Make sure you add the pasta right before eating; the soup can simmer on low for an hour, covered, if you wish, before you add the pasta. When you're ready, add the pasta to the soup and cook for 10 to 12 minutes, stirring occasionally, until the pasta is al dente. Toss in the spinach. Taste and season with more salt and pepper if needed. You can remove the Parmesan rind or leave it in the soup for flavor (just make sure it doesn't end up in someone's bowl).

Serve the soup with freshly shaved Parmesan.

10-MINUTE MEAL PREP

❷ You can chop your onion, garlic, carrots, and squash and store them together in the fridge before using.

NOTE

If you're making this soup and planning on leftovers, I'd suggest cooking the pasta separately. You may need 1 cup less stock. Add the cooked pasta into the soup when reheating to eat. Likewise, if you're making this to freeze, make the soup without the pasta (or transfer half to a freezer container before adding half of the pasta and eating).

HOMEMADE RAMEN NOODLE CUP

SERVES 1 | TIME: 25 MINUTES

I didn't discover those 99-cent packs of ramen until I was at least 13 years old. My mom would groan as I'd throw them in the cart at the grocery store, but she never said no. It was one thing I could easily make myself, so she'd buy me a few.

These days, my ramen cups look a lot different. I still like to use classic ramen noodles, but I add whatever ingredients I can grab in the fridge.

Instead of boiling the noodles in water, I like to use stock and infuse it with a few savory flavors, like soy sauce and hoisin, for a major boost in flavor. Simply break apart the noodles and add them to the jar with some greens, mushrooms, and scallions. Pour the hot stock on top and let it sit for 5 minutes. Instant noodle cups!

1 package of ramen noodles, broken into pieces

½ cup chopped greens, like kale, spinach, or bok choy

¼ cup sliced scallions

¼ cup shiitake mushrooms, sliced

1 to 2 sheets nori, torn into pieces

2 cups vegetable stock

2 tablespoons soy sauce

1½ tablespoons hoisin sauce

Toasted sesame oil, for drizzling

¼ cup chopped fresh cilantro

Pinch of sesame seeds

In a jar, place the dried noodles, greens, scallions, mushrooms, and nori.

In a saucepan, combine the stock, soy sauce, and hoisin and heat until simmering. Once hot, pour the liquid over the ingredients in the jar. Cover and let the jar sit for 3 to 5 minutes, untouched. The noodles should soften.

Stir the soup to combine. Drizzle with sesame oil and top with cilantro and sesame seeds. Eat up!

10-MINUTE MEAL PREP

❶ You can infuse the stock ahead of time and store it in the fridge. Just reheat when ready to eat.

BAKED SWEET POTATO SOUP

SERVES 4 | TIME: 30 MINUTES

I lived for baked potato soup when I was a kid. Sure, it was probably because of the cheese and bacon, but I think it was also because potatoes were my favorite food all around.

This is my grown-up version of that! Sweet potato soup—savory, a little smoky, creamy or with texture (depending how you like it), but still silky and melts in your mouth.

Be sure to bake the sweet potatoes ahead of time—even a few days ahead! They need an hour to bake, but it's all hands-off time and once done, this soup comes together in 30 minutes and is loaded with flavor.

2 tablespoons unsalted butter

½ sweet onion, diced

3 garlic cloves, minced

Kosher salt and freshly cracked black pepper

½ teaspoon smoked paprika

1½ tablespoons all-purpose flour

5 to 6 cups low-sodium vegetable stock

3 baked sweet potatoes, cubed (see Note)

⅓ cup half-and-half

2 scallions, thinly sliced, for topping

¼ cup crumbled goat cheese, for topping

Crumbled bacon or your favorite nuts, for topping (optional)

Heat a large pot over medium-high heat. Add the butter and once melted, stir in the onion, garlic, 1 teaspoon each of salt and pepper, and the smoked paprika. Cook for 5 minutes. Stir in the flour and cook for another 5 minutes, until it's golden and fragrant.

Stream in 5 cups of stock while stirring continuously. Stir in the potatoes and bring the soup to a boil. Reduce to a simmer and cook for 15 minutes, stirring often—especially scraping the bottom. The potatoes will begin to break down; if they are not as broken down as you'd like, mash a bit more with a fork. If the soup is still thick, you can stir in some of the remaining stock.

Carefully transfer the soup to a blender (if you have a small blender, this may need to be done in batches) or use an immersion blender to puree it. You can also keep the soup as is, with chunks of sweet potato. Taste the soup and season with more salt and pepper if needed. Stir in the half-and-half.

Serve hot with the scallions, goat cheese, and crumbled bacon, if using.

10-MINUTE MEAL PREP

- Definitely bake the sweet potatoes ahead of time! If you do, this soup comes together easily in 30 minutes!

- The entire soup can be made ahead of time and leftovers are great.

NOTE

To bake the perfect sweet potatoes, preheat the oven to 425°F. Poke the potatoes with a fork in a few places and bake for 45 to 60 minutes, until tender. Let cool completely, then remove the skins and cut the potatoes into cubes or pieces.

TUSCAN CHEESE TORTELLINI SOUP

SERVES 4 | TIME: 30 MINUTES

Cheese tortellini has become one of my most-used ingredients since having kids. It's so versatile and satisfying, not to mention super easy to use. Add it to almost anything—like this Tuscan tortellini soup—and you get an instant boost!

 With a sun-dried tomato base, plenty of greens, and a few handfuls of tortellini, this is a comforting, filling, and easy weeknight soup. You can throw it together in no time!

4 tablespoons unsalted butter

1 sweet onion, diced

3 carrots, chopped

2 garlic cloves, minced

1 (3-ounce) jar sun-dried tomatoes, drained and chopped

½ teaspoon kosher salt

½ teaspoon freshly cracked black pepper

½ teaspoon dried basil

¼ cup all-purpose flour

6 cups vegetable stock

1 (16-ounce) package cheese tortellini

½ cup half-and-half

1 head of Tuscan kale or Swiss chard, chopped or shredded

Chopped fresh herbs, such as basil or parsley, to garnish

Heat a large pot over medium heat and add the butter. Add in the onion, carrots, garlic, sun-dried tomatoes, salt, pepper, and dried basil. Cook, stirring often, until softened, about 5 minutes.

Stir in the flour to create a roux. It will stick to the veggies and you want the flour to become golden and fragrant after 5 minutes—stir often. Slowly stream in the stock, stirring from the bottom so all the flavor bits get mixed in.

Bring the mixture a boil and add the tortellini. Cook for 5 minutes, until the tortellini soften and are tender enough to eat. Stream in the half-and-half and stir in the chopped greens. Cook for another 5 to 10 minutes, until the kale softens slightly and the soup thickens.

Serve immediately with fresh herbs for garnish!

10-MINUTE MEAL PREP

● The onion, carrots, garlic, and sun-dried tomatoes can be chopped ahead of time and stored together in the fridge.

● The greens can be washed and chopped ahead of time and stored separately in the fridge.

NOTE

If making this for meal prep or leftovers, or you simply don't think it will all get eaten at once, cook the tortellini separately. Store it in its own container and add it to the bowls of soup before reheating. This way it will not soak up all the broth!

ROASTED RED PEPPER SOUP
with pepita granola crunch

SERVES 4 | TIME: 45 MINUTES

Years ago, I used to pour red pepper soup out of a carton and eat it for lunch. I would have it with grilled cheese or a salad and while I liked it, it's only because it was the best option for lunch that day. Mostly, it was always just . . . missing something. Like it needed an extra pinch of salt, a squeeze of fresh lemon or lime, and something most definitely sprinkled on top. Give me the crunch!

That situation has been solved, given that I now make my own roasted red pepper soup that is ANYTHING but boring.

The flavor of the soup alone is delish, but while the soup simmers, I love to pan-crisp halloumi cheese to use for croutons. And then I make a 5-minute pepita granola for sprinkling on top, because the crunch is everything.

4 red bell peppers, chopped

2 tablespoons plus 1 to 2 teaspoons extra-virgin olive oil

Kosher salt and black pepper

1 sweet onion, diced

3 garlic cloves, minced

¼ cup dry sherry

4 cups vegetable stock

1 (8-ounce) block halloumi cheese, sliced

⅓ cup heavy cream

Pepita Granola Crunch (recipe follows)

10-MINUTE MEAL PREP

- The peppers can be roasted ahead of time and stored in the fridge.

- The halloumi can be made ahead of time and stored in the fridge, then reheated before serving.

- The granola can be made ahead of time and stored in the fridge or pantry.

- The entire soup can be made ahead of time—leftovers are wonderful!

Preheat the oven to 425°F. Place the chopped peppers on a baking sheet and toss with 1 tablespoon of the olive oil and a sprinkle of salt and black pepper. Roast for 20 minutes.

In a pot, heat the other tablespoon of olive oil over medium-low heat. Add the onion and garlic with ½ teaspoon each of salt and pepper and cook until softened, about 5 minutes. Stir in the roasted peppers. Add in the sherry and cook for 2 more minutes. Stir in the stock. Bring the mixture to a boil, then reduce it to a simmer. Cook uncovered for 15 minutes.

While the soup simmers, make the halloumi croutons: Heat a nonstick skillet over medium-high heat. Pat the halloumi dry with a paper towel. Add 1 to 2 teaspoons of olive oil to the skillet. Add the halloumi and cook until golden brown, about 2 to 3 minutes per side. Remove the halloumi and place it on a plate. I like to cut the slices in half so they resemble croutons.

Use an immersion blender or carefully transfer the soup to a blender and puree until smooth. Pour it back in the pot and stir in the cream. Taste and season with salt and pepper if needed.

Serve with a sprinkle of the pepita granola crunch and the halloumi croutons on top.

NOTE

This soup freezes great for up to 3 months.

pepita granola crunch

2 teaspoons extra-virgin olive oil

½ cup raw, unsalted pepitas

3 tablespoons old-fashioned oats

1 teaspoon honey

½ teaspoon dried oregano
or basil

¼ teaspoon smoked paprika

¼ teaspoon kosher salt

¼ teaspoon freshly cracked
black pepper

¼ teaspoon crushed red pepper
flakes

In a skillet, heat the olive oil over medium heat.
Add the pepitas and oats and toss. Cook, stirring
often, for 2 to 3 minutes or so until it all begins to
toast. Drizzle in the honey, then add the oregano,
smoked paprika, salt, black pepper, and red
pepper flakes. Toss and stir until everything
comes together. Remove from the heat and
spread the granola on parchment until cooled.

THE GRAIN BOWL FORMULA

SERVES 1, IS EASILY MULTIPLIED | TIME: 30 MINUTES OR LESS

I've never been great at math, but this is one equation that I can solve every time.

Grain bowls are one of my go-to easy weeknight dinners. Partly because you can prep ALL the ingredients ahead of time and combine and eat within minutes. Partly because they are so versatile that you can usually please almost anyone with a combination of grains, vegetables, cheese, and sauce.

And mostly because they are insanely delicious, satisfying, and make for great leftovers.

This is my preferred grain bowl formula, but of course you can add whatever you like. I love to use roasted vegetables for their caramelly sweetness, but raw or fermented work well, too. Use your favorite kind of cheese, nuts for some crunch and satiety, and a dressing or sauce to add a little extra flavor.

Mix it all up and go to town!

1 cup of your favorite cooked grains, such as rice, farro, or couscous

1 to 2 cups chopped vegetables (roasted, grilled, sautéed, fermented, or raw)

3 tablespoons chopped nuts or seeds

1 to 2 ounces grated cheese, if desired

3 to 4 tablespoons of your favorite dressing or sauce

In a large bowl, toss together the grains, vegetables, nuts, and cheese, if using. Drizzle with the dressing.

10-MINUTE MEAL PREP

- Both the grains and vegetables can be prepared ahead of time and stored in the fridge.

- The dressing or sauce can be made ahead of time and stored in the fridge.

CHIPOTLE AND BEER TWO-BEAN VEGETARIAN CHILI

SERVES 4 TO 6 | TIME: 35 MINUTES

I didn't think there would be a meatless chili that would impress Eddie but hey, there's a first time for everything. This chili is HEARTY—in fact, it's impressively chunky and satisfying. Like many of my favorite soups, this is an ideal clean-out-the-fridge meal, meaning the options are almost endless as to what you can add!

The toppings totally MAKE this soup. Please don't skip the Cheddar cheese as it mingles fabulously with the chipotles. A dollop of plain Greek yogurt or sour cream takes the edge off the heat. And a sprinkling of chives and a spritz of lime give it a bright, refreshing punch.

2 tablespoons extra-virgin olive oil

2 bell peppers, diced

1 red onion, diced

1 sweet potato, peeled and chopped

1 chipotle pepper (from a can), diced

1 cup chopped carrot

4 garlic cloves, minced

½ teaspoon kosher salt

½ teaspoon black pepper

2 tablespoons chili powder

1 tablespoon ground cumin

1 tablespoon smoked paprika

1 teaspoon dried oregano

3 tablespoons tomato paste

2 tablespoons adobo sauce from the can of chipotle peppers

1 cup beer

1 (14-ounce) can diced fire roasted tomatoes

1 (28-ounce) can crushed tomatoes

1 (14-ounce) can pinto beans, drained and rinsed

1 (14-ounce) can kidney beans, drained and rinsed

1 cup vegetable stock

Cheddar cheese, for serving

Plain Greek yogurt or sour cream, for serving

Fresh chives, for topping

Lime wedges, for spritzing

In a large pot, heat the olive oil over medium heat and add the bell peppers, onion, sweet potato, chipotle pepper, carrots, garlic, salt, and black pepper. Cook, stirring often, until the vegetables start to soften, about 10 minutes. Stir in the chili powder, cumin, smoked paprika, oregano, tomato paste, and adobo sauce. Cook for 5 minutes more.

Stir in the beer, fire roasted tomatoes, crushed tomatoes, pinto beans, kidney beans, and stock. Bring to a boil, then reduce to a simmer. Cover and cook for 20 minutes. You can simmer for hours if you wish!

Serve with Cheddar cheese, yogurt, chives, and lime wedges.

10-MINUTE MEAL PREP

❶ You can chop the bell peppers, onion, garlic, potato, and carrots 24 hours ahead of time and store in a bag together in the fridge.

❷ You can make this entire meal ahead of time because it only gets more flavorful as it sits.

ROASTED SWEET POTATOES
with honey ginger chickpeas and tahini

SERVES 4 | TIME: 45 MINUTES

When I was a tween, I developed an obsession with Wendy's baked potatoes. The broccoli Cheddar potato was my favorite, which was crazy because I didn't even care for broccoli back then. To absolutely no one's surprise, I would eat around most of the broccoli and scoop up spoonfuls of potatoes covered in cheese sauce.

That's where my love of the stuffed potato began. Now I love to take a baked sweet potato and drizzle it with sauce and stuff it with whatever I have on hand. Sort of like a grain bowl, but inside a sweet potato!

Here, we're drizzling a warm sweet potato with nutty, creamy tahini sauce. It practically tastes like dessert. Then I like to top the whole thing with honey ginger chickpeas that have been toasted in a skillet. Chopped cilantro on top lends the dish a fresh, bright flavor.

4 sweet potatoes

2 to 3 tablespoons extra-virgin olive oil

Kosher salt and black pepper

2 (14-ounce) cans chickpeas, drained, rinsed, and patted dry

2 tablespoons honey

2 garlic cloves, minced

2 tablespoons freshly grated ginger

¼ cup Tahini Sauce (page 41), for serving

2 tablespoons chopped fresh cilantro, for serving

Preheat the oven to 425°F. Line a baking sheet with foil or parchment paper.

Scrub the sweet potatoes and dry them completely. Rub the outsides with 1 tablespoon of the olive oil and cover them with salt and pepper. Place the potatoes on the prepared baking sheet and bake for 45 minutes, until caramelly on the bottoms and super soft.

While the potatoes are baking, make the chickpeas. In a bowl, toss together the chickpeas, honey, garlic, ginger, and ½ teaspoon each of salt and pepper.

Heat a skillet over medium heat and add 1 tablespoon of the olive oil. Once hot, add in the chickpeas and toss to coat. Cook, stirring often, until the chickpeas begin to get crisp and golden, about 8 to 10 minutes. If the chickpeas appear too dry in the pan, drizzle in another tablespoon of olive oil.

Remove the potatoes from the oven and let them cool just slightly. While they are still warm, gently slice them open and drizzle the insides with some of the tahini sauce. Top with the chickpeas and add another drizzle of sauce if you'd like. Sprinkle with the cilantro and serve.

10-MINUTE MEAL PREP

- Fully cook the sweet potatoes ahead of time. Store in the fridge and reheat before eating.

- The chickpeas can be made ahead of time, they will just not be as crispy.

SMOKY BBQ BAKED BLACK BEAN BURGERS

MAKES 8 BURGERS | TIME: 30 MINUTES

Okay, so don't freak out, but I'm going to tell you to BAKE your burgers. I know, it sounds crazy! But let's be real: The biggest plus to baking instead of pan-frying is that they won't crumble in the pan.

The burgers are smoky and have great texture. Once baked, you sandwich them between a bun and slather them with a bunch of guacamole. Sounds like the best idea ever, right?

1 tablespoon extra-virgin olive oil

1 shallot, diced

1 bell pepper, diced

2 garlic cloves, minced

Pinch of kosher salt and black pepper

2 (14-ounce) cans black beans, drained and rinsed

½ cup seasoned bread crumbs

1 teaspoon smoked paprika

½ teaspoon ground cumin

2 tablespoons barbecue sauce, plus more for serving

1 tablespoon Worcestershire sauce

2 large eggs

8 buns, toasted

Quick and Easy Guacamole (page 39), for serving

Microgreens or spring greens, for serving

Preheat the oven to 350°F. Line a baking sheet with parchment paper.

Heat a skillet over medium-low heat and add the olive oil. Add the shallot, bell pepper, garlic, salt, and black pepper and cook until softened, about 5 minutes. Turn off the heat.

Place about three-quarters of the black beans in a large bowl and mash them with a fork or a potato masher. Add the remaining black beans, the shallot/bell pepper mixture, the bread crumbs, smoked paprika, and cumin. Stir to combine. Stir in the barbecue sauce, Worcestershire sauce, and eggs. Form the mixture into 8 patties. Place each patty on the prepared baking sheet.

Bake for 12 minutes. Gently flip (using a spatula and your hand!) and bake for 12 to 15 minutes more. Serve immediately on buns with a drizzle of barbecue sauce, guacamole, and greens.

10-MINUTE MEAL PREP

- The burgers can be formed ahead of time and wrapped in plastic wrap separately, then stored in the fridge. Bake when ready!

BROCCOLI FRITTERS
with chipotle yogurt

MAKES ABOUT 10 FRITTERS | TIME: 35 MINUTES

I've become a little nutty over broccoli and it helps that my kids enjoy it, too. The little trees are one of the first foods I ever served them, and it kind of just stuck!

While 95 percent of the time I'm roasting broccoli with Parmesan (page 246), I do like to prepare it in unique and exciting ways, too.

These broccoli fritters are crisp on the edges and full of flavor. We love to dip them in chipotle yogurt for an extra bite!

3 to 4 cups broccoli florets

2 large eggs, lightly beaten

½ cup all-purpose flour

½ cup finely grated Cheddar cheese

Pinch of crushed red pepper flakes

½ teaspoon garlic powder

¼ teaspoon kosher salt

¼ teaspoon freshly cracked black pepper

2 to 3 tablespoons olive oil

Chipotle Yogurt Sauce (below)

Fill a skillet or saucepan with 1 inch of water and heat it over medium heat. Once simmering, add the broccoli and cover the pan. Steam the broccoli for 3 to 4 minutes, just until it's bright green and slightly tender. Strain the broccoli.

Chop the broccoli into small pieces. Mash half of the pieces with a fork or potato masher.

In a large bowl, stir together the eggs, flour, cheese, red pepper flakes, garlic powder, salt, and black pepper. Fold in the mashed broccoli and the broccoli pieces.

Heat a large nonstick skillet over medium heat. Add 1 tablespoon of the olive oil. Once the oil is hot, drop ½-cup scoops of the broccoli mixture onto the pan. Cook for 2 to 3 minutes per side until golden and crispy. Repeat with the remaining olive oil and broccoli mixture.

Serve immediately with the chipotle yogurt!

chipotle yogurt sauce

10-MINUTE MEAL PREP

- Steam the broccoli ahead of time.
- Make the broccoli fritter mixture 24 hours ahead of time and store it in the fridge.

½ cup plain Greek yogurt

1 tablespoon mayonnaise

1 garlic clove, minced

1 chipotle pepper (from a can), diced

1 tablespoon adobo sauce from the can of chipotle peppers

In a small bowl, whisk together the yogurt, mayonnaise, garlic, chipotle, and adobo sauce until combined.

ROASTED KABOCHA BOWLS
with halloumi and pomegranate

SERVES 4 | TIME: 30 MINUTES

Kabocha squash is a real diamond in the rough. It's sweet and becomes caramelly when roasted. The flavor is almost nutty and it's difficult to not eat it straight out of the oven.

Perhaps my favorite thing about it is that I roast slices with the skin on! Yes, yes, yes. The skin becomes chewy, but in a wonderful way. I love that I can eat the entire slice.

This is a satisfying and hearty grain bowl to throw together. I often like to use leftover ingredients, so if I've roasted squash the night before and have some grains on hand, I'll make it. The little pomegranate seeds give the dish a tangy pop of sweetness and the tahini is a savory, creamy addition that brings everything together.

And the best part? This is great served both warm and cold!

1 kabocha squash, seeds removed and sliced

Olive oil

Pinch of kosher salt and black pepper

Pinch of freshly grated nutmeg

1 (8-ounce) block halloumi cheese, sliced into ½-inch cubes

1½ cups cooked farro or quinoa

½ cup pomegranate seeds

3 tablespoons roasted, salted pepitas

3 tablespoons chopped fresh herbs, like parsley or mint

Lemon wedges, for spritzing

3 tablespoons Tahini Sauce (page 41), for drizzling

Preheat the oven to 425°F.

Place the squash on a baking sheet and drizzle it with a tablespoon of olive oil. Sprinkle it with the salt, pepper, and nutmeg. Toss well to combine everything. Roast for 20 to 25 minutes, or until the squash is fork-tender and begins to get caramelly.

To crisp the halloumi, heat a nonstick skillet over medium-high heat. Pat the halloumi dry with a paper towel. Add a drizzle of olive oil to the skillet. Add the halloumi and cook until golden, about 2 to 3 minutes per side. Remove the halloumi and place it on a plate.

Let's make the bowl! Add the grains to a large bowl. Top with the squash, halloumi, pomegranate seeds, pepitas, and herbs. Give the whole thing a spritz of lemon. Taste and season with additional salt and pepper if needed. Drizzle with the tahini sauce.

10-MINUTE
MEAL PREP

- ❷ The squash can be roasted ahead of time and stored in the fridge.

- ❶ The grains can be prepared ahead of time and stored in the fridge.

- ❸ The tahini sauce can be made ahead of time and stored in the fridge.

SWEET AND SPICY GRILLED SWEET POTATO BOWLS

SERVES 2 | TIME: 35 MINUTES

When it comes to produce, grilling changes everything. There aren't many foods that I won't grill. The grill imparts that smoky flavor that is hard to achieve with any other methods of cooking. It's also easier and usually makes less mess in the kitchen, so that's a bonus.

This is a top-notch version of a grain bowl. You're going to take your favorite grain (I'm using quinoa, but rice or couscous works, too) and stir in some pesto until it's green and lovely and wildly flavorful.

Grill sweet potato spears until they are charred and tender, then toss everything together in one bowl. It's comforting and satisfying, and if you want a little bit of a sauce (I always do), I love the avocado herb drizzle. This is also a great meal to prep ahead of time and one where leftovers are superb!

1 cup quinoa, rinsed

2 sweet potatoes, peeled

2 tablespoons olive oil

2 tablespoons honey

½ teaspoon smoked paprika

½ teaspoon crushed red pepper flakes

2 tablespoons Classic Pesto (page 42)

1 cup cooked or fresh sweet corn kernels

⅔ cup chopped cherry tomatoes

Avocado Herb Sauce (page 50), for serving

Heat your grill to medium-high heat for 10 to 15 minutes.

Prepare the quinoa according to the package directions. (This tends to be 2 cups of liquid to 1 cup quinoa.) Bring to a simmer, cover, and cook for 15 minutes. While that's happening, prepare the potatoes.

Slice the sweet potatoes into spears that are all about the same thickness and are similar in size. This helps everything to grill more evenly. Toss the sweet potatoes with the olive oil, honey, smoked paprika, and red pepper flakes.

You want the grill temperature to be 400°F for grilling the potatoes. Place the potato spears directly on the grates. Grill for 10 to 15 minutes, flipping the potatoes every few minutes, until tender.

In a large bowl, toss the cooked quinoa with the pesto until it's combined.

To make the bowl, place the potato spears on top of the quinoa. Top with the corn and the tomatoes. Drizzle with the avocado herb sauce.

10-MINUTE MEAL PREP

- Potatoes can be cut and stored in a bowl of ice water for 24 hours in the fridge.
- Quinoa can be made ahead of time and stored in the fridge.
- Avocado Herb Sauce can be made ahead of time and stored in the fridge.

CRISPY ORANGE CAULIFLOWER
with coconut rice

SERVES 4 | TIME: 40 MINUTES

This super crunchy oven-roasted cauliflower is a family fave. My kids eat it like it's going out of style, which let's be real: It might be. Cauliflower has had a major moment over the last few years, but it was one of the first vegetables I ever really started to enjoy. So, it will always be popular with us.

I love to serve this over coconut rice. The flavor is incredible and almost tropical.

COCONUT RICE

1½ cups jasmine rice

1½ cups canned coconut milk

½ cup coconut water

¼ teaspoon kosher salt

1½ tablespoons coconut oil

2 tablespoons finely shredded, unsweetened coconut

CAULIFLOWER

Olive oil spray

2 large eggs

¾ cup seasoned bread crumbs

⅓ cup panko bread crumbs

3 tablespoons all-purpose flour

1 head of cauliflower, cut into florets

¼ cup honey

3 tablespoons chili garlic sauce

2 tablespoons brown sugar

1 tablespoon soy sauce

2 tablespoons freshly grated orange zest

1 tablespoon orange juice

¼ teaspoon minced garlic

4 scallions, thinly sliced

Preheat the oven to 400°F.

To make the coconut rice: Heat a saucepan over medium-high heat and add the rice, coconut milk, coconut water, and salt. Stir, then bring to a boil. Reduce the heat to low, cover, and cook for about 30 minutes, until the liquid is absorbed. Fluff with a fork, then stir in the coconut oil. Stir in the shredded coconut.

To make the cauliflower: Place a wire rack on a baking sheet (this helps everything stay crispy) and spray it with olive oil spray.

In one bowl, lightly beat the eggs. In a second bowl, stir together the seasoned bread crumbs, panko bread crumbs, and flour. Take each cauliflower floret and dip it in the egg, then dip it in the bread crumb mixture, coating it completely. Place it on the prepared wire rack and repeat with the other florets. Once they are all breaded, spray them with the olive oil spray. This will help the outsides brown!

Roast the cauliflower for 25 minutes, or until it's golden and crunchy.

While the cauliflower is roasting, make the sauce. In a saucepan, heat the honey, chili garlic sauce, brown sugar, soy sauce, orange zest, orange juice, and garlic over medium heat. Whisk to combine. Cook until the mixture bubbles and let it simmer for a minute or two. Remove it from the heat and let it cool. It will thicken as it cools!

Remove the cauliflower from the oven and drizzle it with the sauce. Sprinkle with scallions and serve over the coconut rice.

10-MINUTE MEAL PREP

❶ Make the coconut rice 24 hours ahead of time and store in the fridge.

❷ Cut the cauliflower into florets and store in the fridge.

❸ Whisk together the sauce ingredients and store in the fridge.

THREE SEASONS OF SHEET-PAN GNOCCHI

Fall
Butternut Squash, Brown Butter, and Sage Gnocchi

SERVES 2 OR 3 AS A MEAL, 4 AS A SIDE DISH | TIME: 35 MINUTES

My favorite sheet-pan gnocchi of them all—FALL! Butternut squash, brown butter, and sage are a delicious classic, and one I can't resist. The gnocchi gets a bit crisp but stays pillowy on the inside.

Nonstick cooking spray

1 (16-ounce) package uncooked potato gnocchi

1½ cups butternut squash cubes (about ½ to 1 inch in size)

2 tablespoons extra-virgin olive oil

3 tablespoons chopped fresh sage, plus more for serving

1 teaspoon garlic powder

½ teaspoon kosher salt

½ teaspoon freshly cracked black pepper

3 tablespoons unsalted butter

¼ cup freshly shaved Parmesan cheese

Pinch of crushed red pepper flakes

Preheat the oven to 425°F. Spray a baking sheet with nonstick spray.

Spread the gnocchi and squash out on the prepared baking sheet in a single layer. Drizzle with the olive oil and toss. Sprinkle with the sage, garlic powder, salt, and pepper. Toss well to combine everything. Make sure everything is seasoned well!

Roast for 20 to 25 minutes, tossing once or twice during cook time.

While the gnocchi is roasting, brown the butter: In a saucepan, heat the butter over medium-low heat. Whisk constantly as the butter bubbles, for about 5 to 6 minutes. The minute you see brown bits appear on the bottom of the pan, remove the saucepan from the heat.

Serve the gnocchi immediately. Drizzle with the brown butter. Sprinkle with the Parmesan, red pepper flakes, and a sprinkling of extra sage.

10-MINUTE MEAL PREP _____

➊ Cut the squash ahead of time and store in the fridge until ready to use.

Tomato Basil Gnocchi

SERVES 2 OR 3 AS A MEAL, 4 AS A SIDE DISH | TIME: 35 MINUTES

This classic flavor combo brings a comforting yet fresh taste to this summer dish. The tomatoes burst and sort of make their own sauce. Heck, you can make it any time of year.

Nonstick cooking spray

1 (16-ounce) package uncooked potato gnocchi

1½ cups grape tomatoes, some cut in half

3 tablespoons extra-virgin olive oil

¼ cup Classic Pesto (page 42)

1 teaspoon garlic powder

½ teaspoon kosher salt

½ teaspoon freshly cracked black pepper

½ teaspoon dried oregano

½ teaspoon dried basil

Pinch of crushed red pepper flakes, plus extra for garnish

¼ cup freshly shaved Parmesan cheese, for topping

Sprinkle of chopped fresh basil, for topping

Preheat your oven to 425°F. Spray a baking sheet with nonstick spray.

Spread the gnocchi and tomatoes out on the prepared baking sheet in a single layer. Drizzle with the olive oil and toss. Spoon on the pesto and toss until everything is coated. Sprinkle with the garlic powder, salt, pepper, oregano, dried basil, and red pepper flakes and toss well to combine everything. Make sure everything, especially the gnocchi, is seasoned well!

Roast for 20 to 25 minutes, tossing once during cook time.

Serve the gnocchi immediately. Sprinkle with the Parmesan, additional red pepper flakes, and fresh basil!

10-MINUTE MEAL PREP

- Prepare the pesto ahead of time and store it in the fridge.
- Grate the cheese ahead of time and store it in the fridge.

Spring

Lemon, Pea, Arugula, and Black Pepper Gnocchi

SERVES 2 OR 3 AS A MEAL, 4 AS A SIDE DISH | TIME: 35 MINUTES

This spring version of my sheet-pan gnocchi is bright and lemony with fresh arugula and peas.

Nonstick cooking spray

1 (16-ounce) package uncooked potato gnocchi

3 tablespoons extra-virgin olive oil

Grated zest and juice of 1 lemon

1 teaspoon garlic powder

½ teaspoon kosher salt

½ teaspoon freshly cracked black pepper

⅔ cup fresh or frozen peas (both work)

2 cups baby arugula

¼ cup freshly shaved Parmesan cheese, for topping

Pinch of crushed red pepper flakes

Sprinkle of chopped fresh herbs, such as parsley, basil or mint, if desired

Preheat your oven to 425°F. Spray a baking sheet with nonstick spray.

Spread the gnocchi out on the prepared baking sheet in a single layer. Drizzle with the olive oil and toss. Sprinkle with the lemon zest, garlic powder, salt, and black pepper. Toss well to combine everything. Make sure everything is seasoned well!

Roast for 20 minutes, tossing once during cook time. Remove the pan from the oven and toss in the peas and arugula. Roast for 5 minutes more.

Serve the gnocchi immediately. Sprinkle with the lemon juice, Parmesan, red pepper flakes, and fresh herbs, if using.

10-MINUTE MEAL PREP

➊ Grate the cheese ahead of time and store it in the fridge.

CHEATER'S TOMATO PIE

SERVES 2 AS A MEAL, 4 AS A SIDE DISH | TIME: 35 MINUTES

We already know that my love for puff pastry has no boundaries. This cheater's tomato pie uses classic flavors—lots of ricotta and tons of fresh basil—but with the ease of puff pastry. It allows the dish to come together quicker and makes it a little more foolproof.

Served with a glass of chilled pinot grigio, this is the epitome of summer. Take me there!

1 sheet frozen puff pastry, thawed

¾ cup ricotta cheese

¼ cup grated Parmesan cheese

½ cup grated Cheddar cheese

2 garlic cloves, minced

Kosher salt and freshly cracked black pepper

2 heirloom tomatoes, sliced

2 tablespoons chopped fresh herbs, like basil

Balsamic glaze, for drizzling (optional)

Preheat the oven to 425°F. Place the puff pastry on a baking sheet.

In a medium bowl, stir together the ricotta, Parmesan, Cheddar, garlic, and ½ teaspoon each of salt and pepper. Spread the ricotta mixture on the puff pastry, leaving a 1-inch border along the edges. Top with the tomatoes and sprinkle on a pinch of salt and pepper.

Bake for 25 to 30 minutes, or until the crust is golden. Top with the fresh herbs, drizzle with balsamic glaze, if using, slice, and serve.

10-MINUTE MEAL PREP

❶ This meal doesn't have much prep, just be sure to thaw your puff pastry according to the package instructions. You can also stir together the ricotta mixture and store it in the fridge.

PUFF PASTRY PIZZAS, TWO WAYS VEGGIE EDITION

Oh puff pastry, just let me count the ways!

Two of my favorite veggie pizza combinations can be found here. We have one that's light and lemony and another that's comforting, loaded with mushrooms and fontina.

Zucchini, Lemon, and Goat Cheese Puff Pastry Pizza

SERVES 2 TO 4 | TIME: 35 MINUTES

1 zucchini, very thinly sliced

Kosher salt

1 sheet frozen puff pastry, thawed

½ cup freshly grated mozzarella cheese

¼ teaspoon black pepper

½ teaspoon garlic powder

4 ounces goat cheese

¼ teaspoon crushed red pepper flakes

Freshly grated zest of 1 lemon

Chopped fresh herbs, such as basil or parsley, for topping

Preheat the oven to 425°F. Line a baking sheet with parchment paper.

Place the zucchini on a cutting board and sprinkle it with salt. Let sit for 5 minutes, then pat it dry with a paper towel. This helps to remove excess moisture.

Place the puff pastry on the prepared baking sheet. Cover with the mozzarella cheese, leaving a 1-inch border. Top with the zucchini and sprinkle with a little more salt, the black pepper, and the garlic powder. Crumble the goat cheese over the zucchini and sprinkle on the red pepper flakes and the lemon zest.

Bake for 20 to 25 minutes, or until golden and crisp. Sprinkle with fresh herbs before slicing and serving.

10-MINUTE MEAL PREP

● Grate the cheese ahead of time and store it in the fridge.

Mushroom, Fontina, and Balsamic Puff Pastry Pizza

SERVES 2 TO 4 | TIME: 35 MINUTES

1 sheet frozen puff pastry, thawed

1½ cups freshly grated fontina cheese

2 cups cremini mushrooms, stems removed, thinly sliced

½ teaspoon freshly cracked black pepper

¼ teaspoon garlic powder

Balsamic glaze, for drizzling

2 tablespoons shaved Parmesan cheese, for topping

2 tablespoons chopped fresh herbs, like basil or chives, for topping

Preheat the oven to 425°F. Line a baking sheet with parchment paper.

Place the puff pastry on the prepared baking sheet. Sprinkle 1 cup of the fontina cheese all over the pastry, leaving a 1-inch border. Top with the thinly sliced mushrooms. Sprinkle on the pepper and garlic powder. Top with the remaining fontina.

Bake for 20 to 25 minutes, or until golden and crisp. Drizzle with the balsamic glaze. Top with the Parmesan and herbs. Slice and serve.

10-MINUTE MEAL PREP

❶ Wipe clean and slice the mushrooms, and store in a sealed container in the fridge.

BUCATINI
with roasted broccoli sauce

SERVES 4 | TIME: 30 MINUTES

Okay, by now, you get it. I really love broccoli. But here's the thing! I know not everyone else does.

So, I created this broccoli pesto sauce as a way to turn haters into lovers. You barely roast the broccoli—just until it's soft. Blend it up with lemon and Parmesan and twirl some soft pasta noodles in it until coated.

Before you know it, you're eating broccoli and enjoying it.

1 head broccoli, cut into florets (about 2 to 3 cups)

1 tablespoon plus ¼ cup extra-virgin olive oil

Kosher salt

½ teaspoon black pepper

1 pound bucatini pasta

1 cup baby arugula

½ cup freshly grated Parmesan, plus more for topping

¼ teaspoon crushed red pepper flakes

2 garlic cloves, minced

1 tablespoon freshly squeezed lemon juice

Preheat the oven to 425°F. Place the broccoli on a baking sheet and drizzle with 1 tablespoon of the olive oil. Sprinkle with ½ teaspoon of salt and the pepper. Toss well to combine.

Roast for 10 to 12 minutes, just until the broccoli is beginning to roast. Let it cool slightly once it's done.

Meanwhile, bring a large pot of salted water to a boil and cook your pasta according to the package directions, until it's al dente. Scoop out and reserve about 3 tablespoons of the pasta cooking water. Once the noodles are done, drain them and place in a large bowl or back in the pot.

Transfer the broccoli to a food processor. Puree with the arugula, Parmesan, ¼ teaspoon salt, ¼ teaspoon black pepper, red pepper flakes, garlic, lemon juice, and the remaining ¼ cup of olive oil. Stream in the reserved pasta cooking water to thin out the sauce.

Pour the broccoli sauce all over the noodles. Toss well until everything is combined. Sprinkle with extra Parmesan and serve.

10-MINUTE MEAL PREP

- ❶ The broccoli can be roasted ahead of time. Do NOT use overly roasted broccoli as it will be bitter.

- ❷ The entire broccoli sauce can be made ahead of time and stored in the fridge.

PUMPKIN RISOTTO

SERVES 4 | TIME: 40 MINUTES

But this is not just any pumpkin risotto! This is brown butter and sage pumpkin risotto. It's the kind of comfort we all need in the fall. Basically, my favorite flavor profile of all time.

I've been on and off the pumpkin train frequently, but one thing is certain: I prefer it much more in savory dishes than I do in sweet dishes. This version is not heavily spiced, so the pumpkin flavor really stands out. It's cozy and cheesy and has sage brown butter swirled in right before serving.

It's like a hug in a bowl.

4 tablespoons unsalted butter

1 handful fresh sage leaves

4 cups vegetable stock, plus more if needed

1 tablespoon extra-virgin olive oil

1 shallot, diced

2 garlic cloves, minced

¼ teaspoon freshly grated nutmeg

¼ teaspoon smoked paprika

Kosher salt and black pepper

1½ cups Arborio rice

1⅓ cups dry white wine

⅔ cup pumpkin puree

½ cup freshly grated Parmesan cheese, plus more for topping

10-MINUTE MEAL PREP _____

❶ You can make the brown butter and sage 24 hours before serving and store them in the fridge. Stir them in at the end of the risotto—it's fine if the brown butter is solid. It will melt!

To make the brown butter and sage: Place 2 tablespoons of the butter in a skillet over medium heat. Cook and let the mixture bubble, stirring occasionally, until brown bits begin to appear on the bottom of the skillet. Add in the sage leaves and cook for 10 seconds. Turn the heat off and continue to cook for about 30 seconds. Remove the sage with kitchen tongs and place on a paper towel to crisp up.

To make the risotto: Heat a saucepan over medium-low heat and add the vegetable stock and cover. Heat until it's simmering. Do not allow to boil; you just want it warm.

Heat a large saucepan or Dutch oven over medium heat. Add in the olive oil and the remaining 2 tablespoons of butter (not the brown butter), then add the shallot, garlic, nutmeg, paprika, and ¼ teaspoon each of salt and pepper. Stir to coat and cook for 2 to 3 minutes until the shallot is soft. Increase the heat slightly and add the rice, stirring to coat. Cook for about 5 minutes, stirring a few times, until the rice is translucent and begins to toast.

Reduce the heat to medium-low and pour in the wine. Continue to stir as the rice absorbs the wine, about 3 to 5 minutes. When most of it is absorbed, add in about a third of the warm vegetable stock. Repeat the process, continuously stirring until the stock is absorbed, then add another third. Repeat until all of the stock is used and absorbed and the rice is cooked, making sure to take a spoonful and taste. The whole process will take about 20 to 25 minutes. If the rice is still too chewy and dense, heat a bit more liquid and add it, continuously stirring. The rule I go by is to add enough liquid just to cover the very top of the risotto.

(recipe continues)

Once the rice is cooked al dente (or to your liking), reduce the heat to low and stir in the pumpkin puree. Take a few minutes and really stir so it is well absorbed. Stir in the Parmesan and the reserved brown butter, mixing to combine. Taste and add more salt and pepper if desired—I usually add at least ½ teaspoon each.

To serve, place the risotto in bowls and top with some additional Parmesan and a sprinkling of the crisped sage leaves.

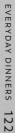

BURRATA BAKED ZITI
with extra veg

SERVES 6 | TIME: 35 MINUTES

Burrata cheese was sent straight from the heavens. It's luscious and creamy and makes everything better.

This baked ziti is stuffed with vegetables—and one of my best tips is that you can use ANY leftover veggies in this recipe! If you have extra vegetables from dinner last night, this is the recipe to make. And if you want to start from scratch, this still comes together in 30 minutes!

Kosher salt

1 pound ziti pasta

1 tablespoon extra-virgin olive oil

1 sweet onion, diced

3 garlic cloves, minced

1 bell pepper, diced

Black pepper

½ teaspoon dried basil

½ teaspoon dried oregano

¼ teaspoon crushed red pepper flakes

1 medium zucchini, diced

1 tablespoon tomato paste

3 tablespoons dry red wine

1 batch of Fire Roasted Marinara (page 41) or 1 (32-ounce) jar marinara sauce

¼ cup finely grated Parmesan cheese

8 ounces freshly grated mozzarella cheese

2 (8-ounce) balls of burrata cheese

Chopped fresh herbs, like basil or parsley, for sprinkling

Preheat the oven to 400°F. Bring a large pot of salted water to a boil and cook the ziti until al dente, according to the package instructions.

While the pasta is cooking, heat a large skillet over medium-low heat and add the olive oil. Add in the onion, garlic, and bell pepper with a big pinch of salt and black pepper. Stir in the dried basil, oregano, and red pepper flakes. Cook for 5 minutes, until the veggies are slightly softened. Stir in the zucchini and cook for 3 minutes more. Stir in the tomato paste and red wine.

Pour the marinara sauce into the skillet. Stir in the Parmesan and mix everything together. By now, the pasta should be finished cooking. Drain the pasta and transfer it to a 9 × 13-inch baking dish. Pour the marinara sauce mixture over the top. Sprinkle on the mozzarella cheese, and toss once or twice to stir it into the pasta.

Break apart the balls of burrata and place the pieces on top of the pasta. Bake for 20 minutes, or until the pasta is golden and bubbly.

10-MINUTE MEAL PREP

- Cook the pasta ahead of time, toss it with olive oil so it doesn't stick together, and store it in the fridge.
- Cook the vegetables ahead of time and store them in the fridge.
- Use any and all roasted vegetables or leftovers for the recipe!

CHEESY LEMON ORZO

SERVES 4 AS A MEAL, 6 AS A SIDE DISH | TIME: 30 MINUTES

This lemon orzo dish, which resembles a super sophisticated mac and cheese, is packed with fresh flavor and will certainly make a statement in your kitchen. Serve it for dinner or as a side dish to chicken or seafood.

1 tablespoon unsalted butter

1 shallot, diced

4 garlic cloves, minced

¼ teaspoon dried basil

Kosher salt and black pepper

1 cup milk

½ cup heavy cream

1 pound orzo, cooked according to package directions and drained

4 ounces freshly grated fontina cheese

4 ounces freshly grated Gruyère cheese

2 ounces freshly grated Parmesan cheese

2 tablespoons freshly grated lemon zest

1 handful fresh basil, torn, for topping

½ teaspoon crushed red pepper flakes

Heat a large saucepan over medium-low heat and add the butter. Stir in the shallot, garlic, dried basil, and ½ teaspoon each of salt and pepper. Cook until the shallot softens, about 5 minutes. Stream in the milk and heavy cream, stirring to combine. Bring the mixture to a simmer, then reduce the heat to low.

Stir the cooked orzo into the milk mixture. Once combined, stir in the grated fontina, Gruyère, and Parmesan cheeses and toss to combine. Cook, stirring often, for 6 to 8 minutes until the cheese is starting to melt. Stir in the lemon zest. Taste and add more salt and pepper if needed. Top with the fresh basil and the red pepper flakes and serve.

10-MINUTE MEAL PREP

- The orzo can be cooked ahead of time. Once cooked, toss it with a drop of olive oil so it doesn't stick together and store it in the fridge.
- The cheeses can be grated ahead of time and stored in the fridge.

ROASTED ITALIAN WHITE BEANS
with burst tomato spaghetti

SERVES 4 | TIME: 30 MINUTES

White beans are so creamy and rich. When roasted, the outsides become slightly crisp and they are the perfect addition to the burst tomato spaghetti. The tomatoes pop in garlic oil and they're irresistible!

2 (14-ounce) cans cannellini beans, drained and rinsed

1 teaspoon garlic powder

1 teaspoon dried Italian seasoning

½ teaspoon crushed red pepper flakes

4 tablespoons extra-virgin olive oil

Kosher salt and black pepper

1 pound spaghetti

4 garlic cloves, minced

16 ounces cherry tomatoes

Fresh basil, for garnish

Preheat the oven to 425°F.

Pat the beans completely dry. In a small bowl, stir together the garlic powder, Italian seasoning, and red pepper flakes.

Place the beans on a baking sheet and drizzle with 1 tablespoon of the olive oil. Toss to coat. Sprinkle the spice mixture all over, and toss to make sure that all the beans are covered. Roast for 15 to 20 minutes, stirring once during cook time.

While the beans are roasting, bring a pot of salted water to a boil. Cook the pasta according to the directions.

Heat a large skillet over medium heat and add the remaining 3 tablespoons of olive oil. Stir in the garlic. Add the cherry tomatoes and toss. Add a sprinkle of salt and pepper. Cook, stirring occasionally, until the tomatoes begin to burst, about 10 minutes. You can smash a few if desired.

Toss in the drained spaghetti and stir, making sure to coat it all with the olive oil and tomatoes. Stir in the roasted white beans. Top with fresh basil and serve!

10-MINUTE MEAL PREP

- Cook the pasta ahead of time, toss it with olive oil, and store in the fridge.

- Roast the white beans ahead of time and store in the fridge. Reheat in the pasta by stirring beans in the tomato and olive oil mixture when you add it to the pasta.

EMBARRASSINGLY EASY
SCRAMBLED EGG BREAKFAST TACOS
with avocado pico

SERVES 2 | TIME: 20 MINUTES

These tacos are my secret weapon.

They just taste SO good. At the same time, they are ridiculously easy and barely worthy of a written recipe, but I can't hold it in any longer. These make an ideal breakfast, lunch, or dinner. Keep some of the pico in your fridge at all times and you can have these made in just five minutes.

You can also throw in whatever may be left in your fridge! Sometimes you just need a reminder that something as simple as this is everything you want to eat.

1 pint cherry tomatoes, quartered

1 avocado, cubed

½ sweet onion, diced

¼ cup fresh cilantro, chopped

Juice of half a lime

Pinch of kosher salt and black pepper

2 tablespoons unsalted butter

4 large eggs

4 (4-inch) corn or flour tortillas

3 tablespoons crumbled cotija cheese

To make the avocado pico, toss together the tomatoes, avocado, onion, cilantro, and lime juice in a medium bowl. Season with salt and pepper.

Heat a large nonstick skillet over medium-low heat and add 1 tablespoon of butter. Lightly beat the eggs until just combined and then pour in the skillet. Stir and toss until the eggs cook, and right before they firm up, stir in the remaining tablespoon of butter and toss until it's incorporated into the scrambled eggs.

To assemble, add the scrambled eggs to the tortillas and top with the avocado pico. Top with the crumbled cotija and serve.

10-MINUTE MEAL PREP

❶ Make the pico ahead of time, skipping the avocado, and store it in the fridge. Stir in the avocado right before serving.

CACIO E PEPE SPAGHETTI SQUASH

SERVES 2 TO 4 | TIME: 35 MINUTES

A love of black pepper eluded me my entire life until I tried toasting it in butter. Oh yes, turning everything into a version of *cacio e pepe* also helped. The toasty, warm, peppery butter really makes anything taste fantastic.

I love to serve the squash in its own skin, but you can also scrape out the strands and serve this as a side dish!

2 spaghetti squash

1 to 2 tablespoons extra-virgin olive oil

Kosher salt and freshly ground black pepper

4 tablespoons unsalted butter

½ cup freshly grated pecorino cheese, plus extra for sprinkling

Preheat the oven to 400°F. Line a baking sheet with parchment paper or foil.

Slice the spaghetti squash in half widthwise, right down the center. Scrape out the seeds (I like to use a grapefruit spoon for this) and place the halves, cut side down, on the prepared baking sheet. Spritz or brush them with the olive oil and sprinkle with salt and pepper.

Roast the squash for 30 minutes, or until the strands easily scrape away from the sides.

While the squash is roasting, in a saucepan, melt the 4 tablespoons of butter over medium heat. Once it's melted, stir in 2 teaspoons of pepper. Toast for about 60 seconds. Remove from the heat.

Use a fork to scrape the strands of the squash. Evenly distribute the melted pepper butter into each squash half, then add ¼ cup of cheese to each. Stir with your fork to toss and mix everything together, making sure the cheese is dispersed and the strands from the sides and bottom are scraped.

Top with extra pepper and cheese and serve immediately.

10-MINUTE MEAL PREP

❶ The squash can be roasted ahead of time and stored in the fridge. Do not scrape the strands until you reheat and you're ready to finish the dish.

CRISPY TRUFFLED POTATO OMELET

SERVES 2 | TIME: 25 MINUTES

We've already discussed my love of breakfast for dinner, so this should come as no surprise. This is the ultimate egg breakfast, complete with crispy fried potatoes that are sprinkled with truffle salt for some extra umami.

Of course, when left to your own devices you can throw whatever you like in your omelet. Make it a clean-out-the-fridge meal and add vegetables or different cheeses. The key is to fold the crispy potatoes directly inside the omelet. This way you get a bite of crispy potato with cheesy egg all at once and it's such a lovely flavor explosion.

2 tablespoons unsalted butter

1 medium Yukon Gold potato, peeled or unpeeled, diced

Truffle salt

Freshly cracked black pepper

5 large eggs

Pinch of kosher salt

2 ounces freshly grated white Cheddar cheese

2 scallions, thinly sliced

Heat a large nonstick skillet over medium heat and add 1 tablespoon of the butter. Add in the diced potatoes and toss to coat. Add a pinch of the truffle salt and pepper. Cook, tossing occasionally, until the potatoes are crispy, about 10 minutes. Taste one and if you'd like more truffle salt, add it! Transfer the potatoes to a plate.

In a bowl, whisk together the eggs, 2 tablespoons water, and a pinch of kosher salt and pepper.

Using the same skillet, melt the remaining tablespoon of butter over medium-low heat. Once melted, pour the eggs into the skillet. Quickly move a spatula through them to slightly scramble, then let them sit without stirring—occasionally lifting up the edges to let any uncooked egg run into the cracks—for 2 to 3 minutes, until they're set in the center.

Once the center of the omelet is set, sprinkle in the cheese. Add the potatoes in the center along with a sprinkling of scallions. Fold the omelet over. If desired, give it another sprinkle of truffle salt. Serve immediately.

10-MINUTE
MEAL PREP

- Dice the potatoes up to 12 hours ahead of time and keep them stored in a bowl of cold water in the fridge. Pat them dry before cooking.

- Grate the cheese and keep it stored in the fridge.

BAKED EGG BAGUETTE

SERVES 2 TO 4 | TIME: 35 MINUTES

This is sort of like a cheater's frittata served with toast. Except it's all baked in the loaf of bread.

    This is a lovely dish to serve if you're having friends over for brunch. It's toasty and warm and the egg filling is creamy and soft. You can add cooked sausage or bacon to the filling, too, if you'd like. Another great clean-out-the-fridge meal and one we love to make for dinner!

1 petite French baguette, about 8 to 10 inches in length

6 large eggs

1 shallot, diced

1 garlic clove, minced

1 bell pepper, diced

¼ cup half-and-half

½ teaspoon kosher salt

½ teaspoon black pepper

2 tablespoons chopped fresh herbs, like basil or parsley

⅔ cup freshly grated mozzarella or Provolone cheese

Preheat the oven to 400°F.

Place the baguette on a baking sheet, split the baguette lengthwise, and cut the center out of it, leaving about an inch on each end and enough at the sides to hold in the egg mixture.

In a bowl, whisk together the eggs with the shallot, garlic, bell pepper, half-and-half, salt, and pepper. Stir in the herbs and cheese. Pour the egg mixture into the baguette.

Bake for 25 to 30 minutes, or until the eggs are completely set in the center. Let cool for 5 minutes before slicing and serving.

10-MINUTE MEAL PREP

- ❷ Scoop out the center of the baguette ahead of time and store the bread in the fridge.

- ❷ Grate the cheese ahead of time and store it in the fridge.

MINI WHITE PIZZA BAGELS

SERVES 4 | TIME: 30 MINUTES

Welcome to grown-up kid food. When I first told Eddie I was going to make an adult version of pizza bagels, he looked at me like I was crazy. Then he took a bite and instantly regretted his wide eyes.

These are mini pizza bagel versions of my favorite white pizza that we ate when I was a kid. Think tomatoes, lots of garlic, some Parmesan, basil, and oregano. I like to use Fontinella cheese here because it tastes fancy—the flavor is slightly sharp and also nutty, and it melts perfectly.

Make these when you're craving comfort food but want a special version of it. Serve them to everyone you love!

6 mini bagels

Garlic Confit (page 36)

Pinch of kosher salt

6 ounces freshly grated Fontinella cheese

3 beefsteak tomatoes, cut into 12 slices

¼ cup finely grated Parmesan cheese

Freshly cracked black pepper

Fresh oregano and basil, for garnish

Preheat the oven to 400°F.

Slice the bagels in half and place them on a baking sheet, cut sides up. Drizzle them with 1 to 2 tablespoons of oil from the garlic confit. Take a few of the garlic confit cloves and smash them with a fork and a pinch of salt. Spread the smashed cloves on the bagels.

Top each bagel with a sprinkling of Fontinella. Top the cheese with a tomato slice. Add a sprinkling of Parmesan on top along with the pepper.

Bake the bagels for 10 to 15 minutes, until the cheese is golden and bubbly and melted. Garnish with the oregano and basil leaves and eat immediately!

10-MINUTE MEAL PREP

❶ Grate the cheeses ahead of time and store them in the fridge.

SMASHED BROCCOLI FRIED RICE

SERVES 2 | TIME: 25 MINUTES

For a flavorful dish, I definitely think you should take broccoli florets and smash them into a pan, creating crispy crunchy edges. Then, make a faux fried rice with lots of sesame and soy. Toss it all together and throw a fried egg on top, complete with the runny yolk of your dreams.

And because I can't help myself, I occasionally like to add crisped, cooked bacon. It's a fun, flavorful dish, with or without!

1 tablespoon canola oil

2 cups broccoli florets

4 garlic cloves, minced

2 cups cooked brown rice, preferably left over from the day before

4 scallions, sliced

1 or 2 tablespoons soy sauce

2 teaspoons toasted sesame oil, plus extra for drizzling

2 large eggs, fried or poached

Chili garlic paste, for serving

Heat a large skillet or wok over medium heat and add the canola oil.

Stir in the broccoli. Toss well and cook until the broccoli softens, stirring occasionally, about 5 to 6 minutes. Stir in the garlic.

Take a fork or another kitchen tool like a meat tenderizer and smash each broccoli floret into the bottom of the pan.

Increase the heat to medium-high. Add in the rice, tossing to coat, then let it sit for 1 to 2 minutes to crisp up and get golden on the bottom. Repeat this a few times—toss, then let it sit for a minute or two. Stir in the scallions, a tablespoon of the soy sauce, and the sesame oil. Toss, breaking apart any pieces, and let sit for another 1 to 2 minutes. Repeat another 1 or 2 times until the rice is a bit crispy and golden.

At this point, taste the rice and if it needs to be seasoned a bit more, stir in the remaining tablespoon of soy sauce. You can keep your rice over low heat and take a few minutes here to prepare your eggs, whether you fry them or poach them. I love to add a fried egg on top.

Spoon the rice into bowls or plates and top each one with an egg, an extra drizzle of toasted sesame oil, and some chili garlic paste.

10-MINUTE MEAL PREP

❶ Cook the rice and store it in the fridge.

❷ Chop the broccoli into florets and store them in the fridge.

COMFORTING MUSHROOM PASTA
with brown butter sauce

SERVES 2 | TIME: 30 MINUTES

This is an embarrassingly easy but comforting, savory, and crave-worthy pasta dish. You will dream of this after tasting it, I'm sure of it.

Kosher salt

8 ounces pasta

5 tablespoons unsalted butter

12 ounces mixed mushrooms, like cremini and shiitake, sliced

4 garlic cloves, minced

Freshly cracked black pepper

⅓ cup freshly grated Parmesan cheese

Bring a pot of salted water to a boil and cook the pasta according to the package directions.

While the pasta is cooking, make the mushrooms: Heat a large skillet over medium heat and add the butter. Let it bubble and begin to brown, then stir in the mushrooms. Cook, stirring occasionally, until the mushrooms soften and begin to brown, about 6 minutes. Stir in the garlic, and ½ teaspoon each of salt and pepper.

Add the cooked pasta to the skillet, tossing well. Stir in the Parmesan. Taste and season additionally if needed. Serve immediately.

10-MINUTE MEAL PREP

- ❶ Cook the pasta ahead of time, toss it with olive oil, and store it in the fridge.

- ❷ Wash and slice the mushrooms ahead of time and store them in a sealed container in the fridge.

SPINACH LASAGNA ROLL-UPS
with roasted red pepper sauce

SERVES 4 | TIME: 40 MINUTES

Lasagna roll-ups are a great way to get all the delish, comfort flavor of lasagna without making an enormous casserole on a weeknight!

These noodles are filled with spinach and ricotta and rolled into cute spirals, then blanketed with a roasted red pepper sauce. Baked until golden and bubbly, they're incredible when served with a house salad and a slice of garlic bread.

1 batch of Roasted Red Pepper Sauce (page 43)

Kosher salt

12 lasagna noodles

1 tablespoon extra-virgin olive oil

4 garlic cloves, minced

16 ounces fresh baby spinach

16 ounces ricotta cheese

1 large egg

½ cup finely grated Parmesan cheese

Black pepper

⅔ cup freshly grated mozzarella

Fresh chopped basil, to garnish

Preheat the oven to 350°F. (If you haven't made the roasted red pepper sauce yet, start with that!)

Bring a pot of salted water to a boil. Cook the lasagna noodles according to the package instructions. Drain and immediately spread the noodles out on a baking sheet.

Heat a skillet over medium-low heat and add the olive oil. Add in the garlic and the spinach, stirring until the spinach wilts. Cook until all the spinach is wilted.

In a bowl, stir together the ricotta, egg, Parmesan, and salt and pepper to taste.

For each roll-up, spread 1 or 2 tablespoons of the ricotta mixture on a noodle. Top with the sautéed spinach mixture. Top with a few spoonfuls of the red pepper sauce. Roll the noodle up and place it in a baking dish with the seam down. Repeat with remaining noodles.

Once the roll-ups are all in the dish, top with the remaining red pepper sauce and a sprinkling of mozzarella cheese. Bake for 20 minutes or until the cheese is melty and bubbly. Garnish with fresh basil.

10-MINUTE MEAL PREP

❶ Make the red pepper sauce a few days ahead and store it in the fridge.

❷ Cook the lasagna noodles 24 hours ahead, spritz or toss with olive oil so they don't stick, and store them in the fridge.

❸ Make the garlic-spinach mixture a day ahead of time and store in the fridge.

❹ Make the ricotta mixture a day ahead of time and store it in the fridge.

BLACK BEAN
AND AVOCADO BURRITOS

SERVES 4 | TIME: 30 MINUTES

I live for these saucy black beans. I got the recipe from my cousin Lacy—and they make everything taste better! Filling and fantastic, they are a great base for burritos and enchiladas and a tasty addition to tacos. Or make a burrito with freshly cubed avocado and rice! You're going to love it.

2 (14-ounce) cans black beans, drained and rinsed

½ red onion, diced

1 green bell pepper, diced

3 whole garlic cloves

1 teaspoon chili powder

1 teaspoon smoked paprika

½ teaspoon ground cumin

Pinch of cayenne pepper

Pinch of kosher salt

Pinch of freshly cracked black pepper

1 cup low-sodium vegetable stock

Juice of 1 lime

4 (10- to 12-inch) flour tortillas, warmed

1 cup cooked brown rice

½ cup crumbled cotija cheese

2 avocados, diced

Salsa, for serving

In a saucepan, combine the black beans, onion, bell pepper, garlic, chili powder, smoked paprika, cumin, cayenne, salt, and pepper over medium-low heat. Add the stock and lime juice and stir. Simmer the beans, uncovered, stirring occasionally, for 10 to 15 minutes, until the mixture starts to reduce and thicken. Set them aside to cool slightly—the mixture will thicken even more. Remove the garlic cloves from the beans. (If you're making these beans ahead of time, you can store them in a container in the fridge right now!)

To build the burritos, place a scoop of the black beans in the center of each tortilla. Add ¼ cup brown rice, 2 tablespoons of cotija cheese, and a quarter of the avocado cubes to each tortilla. Fold up the bottom of the tortilla, then one side, then the top and the other side.

Serve immediately with your favorite salsa.

**10-MINUTE
MEAL PREP**

❶ Make the black beans ahead of time and store in the fridge. Reheat before filling the burrito.

POULTRY

I find that one of my goals week after week is to make sure we're not eating boring chicken dinners. More often than not we get stuck in the rut of eating the same meals over and over again.

As I've gotten older and succumbed to my Internet-generation ways, I find myself constantly craving new meals and more variety. It's no secret that my husband is a chicken-loving guy who, even when eating one of my delish meatless meals, wonders where the chicken is. He could eat the same chicken dinner probably two or three times a week.

But me? No way.

So, I'm always on a mission to discover new pairings or meals to relieve that boredom and make us look forward to dinner again.

Chicken is so versatile and our favorite cut to use is boneless, skinless chicken thighs. They have a bit more flavor and also don't tend to get as dry as chicken breasts. In most of these recipes, chicken breasts and thighs can be used interchangeably; you just may need to adjust the cook time a bit.

I very much hope this brings some excitement to the dinner table for you! You know, that good, comforting 1993 feeling of the whole family sitting down together.

SUMMER WATERMELON
CHICKEN SALAD

SERVES 2 | TIME: 25 MINUTES

Behold! My favorite chicken salad of ALL time.

Chopped salads make me so happy. There is just something about having a bite of everything on your fork—it's delicious, right?! This salad is the epitome of summertime, albeit a little unique. It's fresh and flavorful, with a hint of smokiness from the grilled chicken. The watermelon is refreshing, sweet, and crunchy. So is the cucumber! The feta is creamy with a slight tang. The pistachios are savory.

And the dressing? Well, that is downright drinkable. A quick chili-lime vinaigrette adds a punch to this salad. The chili + watermelon combination is a wonderful classic, and this modern twist is one that you will want to make weekly, come summertime!

2 boneless, skinless chicken breasts

Kosher salt and black pepper

1 tablespoon extra-virgin olive oil

1 cup cubed watermelon

½ cup sliced cucumber

¼ cup crumbled feta cheese

1 tablespoon diced shallot

Chili-Lime Vinaigrette (page 51)

2 tablespoons chopped pistachios

2 tablespoons chopped fresh herbs, like parsley, dill, or basil

Grill your chicken: Preheat the grill to the highest setting and season the chicken with salt and pepper. Drizzle it with the olive oil and place it on the grates. Grill for 5 to 6 minutes per side, or until the internal temperature reaches 165°F. Chop into cubes. Use 1 cup of the cubed chicken for this salad; save the rest for another time.

In a bowl, combine the chicken (it can be warm or cold), watermelon, cucumber, feta, and shallot. Season with salt and pepper. Drizzle with the vinaigrette and top with the pistachios and fresh herbs.

10-MINUTE MEAL PREP

- Grill the chicken ahead of time. You can also use rotisserie chicken in a pinch.

- You can cut the watermelon ahead of time.

- I prefer to chop the cucumber and shallot right before serving. But feel free to chop the pistachios and store them in the pantry or fridge for a day.

- The vinaigrette can be made and stored in the fridge 2 days ahead of time.

CRISPY PARMESAN CHICKEN WEDGE SALAD

SERVES 2 TO 4 | TIME: 35 MINUTES

Sometimes all it takes to switch things up and make a salad special are the same ingredients, served in different ways.

I'm not an iceberg hater. In fact, I sometimes crave the cool, refreshing bite of iceberg. It pairs so well with my crispy Parmesan chicken, which is easier, less messy, and nearly as crunchy as fried chicken. I love to slice the chicken and serve it next to a seasoned iceberg wedge with lots of herbs.

Drizzling this entire thing in avocado buttermilk dressing takes it over the top. I'm almost always a vinaigrette girl until it comes to buttermilk dressing. The tang is just so good! If you're craving something more tart, the house vinaigrette is wonderful, too.

PARMESAN CHICKEN

High-heat oil spray such as olive oil, grapeseed oil, or coconut oil

2 boneless, skinless chicken breasts

½ teaspoon kosher salt

½ teaspoon black pepper

1 large egg

1 cup seasoned panko bread crumbs

½ cup seasoned fine bread crumbs

⅓ cup freshly grated Parmesan cheese

To make the Parmesan chicken: Preheat the oven to 425°F. Line a baking sheet with foil and place a wire rack on top. Spray the rack with high-heat oil spray and set aside.

Pound the chicken with a meat tenderizer until it is about ¼ to ½ inch in thickness. Season the chicken on both sides with the salt and pepper.

In a small bowl, lightly beat the egg. In a large bowl, combine the panko bread crumbs, the fine bread crumbs, and the Parmesan. Dip each piece of chicken in the beaten egg and then dredge it through the bread crumbs, pressing lightly to adhere.

Place the chicken pieces on the wire rack. Spray each with a mist of the high-heat oil. Bake the chicken for 10 to 12 minutes, remove it from the oven, gently flip each piece and mist with the spray, then bake for 10 to 12 minutes more.

Let the chicken cool slightly, then slice.

10-MINUTE MEAL PREP

- Prepare your dressing ahead of time and store it in the fridge for up to 2 days.

- Combine your bread crumb mixture and store it in the fridge until ready to use.

SALAD

1 large or 2 small heads iceberg lettuce, cut into wedges

Kosher salt and black pepper

Avocado Buttermilk Dressing (page 48) or House Vinaigrette (page 58)

1 cup microgreens, for sprinkling

¼ cup chopped fresh herbs, like chives, basil, and dill

To make the salad: Cut the iceberg lettuce into wedges. Sprinkle with salt and pepper, then drizzle with a bit of the dressing. Add the chicken on top (or next to it!) with a sprinkling of microgreens and herbs. Add more dressing, if desired, and serve.

NOTES

The key to crunchy chicken and keeping the breading on the chicken is the wire rack AND the oil misting spray! This chicken is best when prepared right before eating. Leftovers are good, albeit not as crisp.

BBQ CHICKEN PASTA SALAD

SERVES 4 TO 6 | TIME: 30 MINUTES

In our house, "BBQ chicken" is a flavor combo often thrown around when we're discussing sandwiches, pizza, tacos, or salads. And when we say "BBQ chicken," we mean barbecue sauce, red onions (pickled or plain), bacon, Cheddar cheese, scallions or chives, and maybe corn and cilantro, depending on the season.

If you haven't tried these flavors together before, you are in for a treat. Don't they sound fabulous?!

I love to make a pasta salad that is anything but ordinary. I didn't grow up eating the classic Italian pasta salad or even a creamy macaroni salad. I prefer unexpected flavors like this, and salads with lots of texture that can be considered an entire meal. And BBQ chicken always wins with Eddie, so this makes a frequent appearance in the kitchen.

½ cup barbecue sauce

½ cup plain Greek yogurt

2 tablespoons mayonnaise

1 tablespoon honey

1 pound short cut pasta, like elbows or shells, cooked

1½ cups shredded or cubed cooked chicken

⅔ cup freshly grated or cubed white Cheddar cheese

⅓ cup sliced scallions

1 avocado, cubed

1 cup grape tomatoes, chopped

1 cup cooked or fresh sweet corn kernels

¼ cup cooked and crumbled bacon

¼ cup Quick Pickled Onions (page 35)

½ cup chopped fresh cilantro

In a bowl, whisk together the barbecue sauce, yogurt, mayonnaise, and honey.

In a large bowl, combine the cooked pasta with the barbecue sauce mixture. Toss in the shredded chicken, cheese, scallions, avocado, tomatoes, corn, bacon, and pickled onions.

Toss the ingredients until combined. Sprinkle on some fresh cilantro and toss once more. Serve!

10-MINUTE MEAL PREP _____

● A day or two ahead of time, you can prep all the ingredients and store them separately in the fridge. Stir together your dressing, and cook the pasta, chicken, and bacon. Grate your cheese and chop your tomatoes. Combine everything together in the bowl before serving.

NOTE _____

Leftovers of this pasta salad are wonderful! They are not as saucy or creamy as on the first day, but they still taste fantastic. You can keep this in the fridge for 2 to 3 days.

CHICKEN TORTILLA SOUP

SERVES 4 | TIME: 30 MINUTES

Tortilla soup is the ultimate comfort food—creamy, cheesy, hearty, and flavorful. And I come from a long line of tortilla soup lovers—my grandmother adored it. It's still my mom's favorite. So, it's only natural that it's one of my go-to soups.

I love this recipe so much because the soup is thickened with actual corn tortillas, not a flour roux or cream. It comes together fairly quickly but also packs a ton of flavor—which is super-nice for a weeknight! No need to stand over the stove for three hours to get a developed flavor. And you'll find that leftovers are just as wonderful.

Toppings are where I shine when it comes to weeknight soups. I love to make a toppings bar, be it large or small. Think about what would end up on your tacos . . . then throw it on your soup. Tortilla chips, cilantro, tomatoes, scallions, cotija cheese—the options are endless and totally up to you!

2 tablespoons extra-virgin olive oil

1 sweet onion, diced

4 garlic cloves, minced

2 teaspoons ground cumin

1 teaspoon smoked paprika

Kosher salt and black pepper

1 (14-ounce) can fire roasted diced tomatoes

4 cups low-sodium chicken stock

4 (4-inch) corn tortillas, cut into pieces

4 ounces freshly grated Monterey Jack cheese

4 ounces freshly grated sharp Cheddar cheese, plus extra for topping

8 ounces cooked and shredded chicken

For topping: diced avocado, thinly sliced radish, tortilla chips, lime wedges, chopped fresh cilantro

Heat a large pot over medium-low heat and add the olive oil. Stir in the onion, garlic, cumin, smoked paprika, and ½ teaspoon each of salt and pepper. Cook until the onion softens, about 5 to 6 minutes. Pour in the diced tomatoes and chicken stock and add the tortilla pieces. Bring the mixture to a boil, then reduce it to a simmer and cover. Simmer for 5 minutes.

Carefully transfer the mixture to a blender and puree until smooth. You could also use an immersion blender, but I find that they spray everywhere. Pour the soup back into the pot and heat it over low heat. Stir in the Monterey Jack and Cheddar cheeses, one handful at a time, until melted. Stir in the chicken. Cook on low until the soup is heated through. Taste and season additionally if needed.

Serve in bowls and top with extra Cheddar, avocado, radish, tortilla chips, lime wedges, and cilantro.

10-MINUTE MEAL PREP

- This soup can be made a day or so in advance—the flavors just get better!

- If you want to make it fresh, chop your onion, grate your cheeses, and shred your chicken ahead of time, storing them separately in the fridge.

- You can combine the necessary spices and keep them in the pantry until needed.

NOTE

The soup freezes well for up to 3 months. Thaw in the fridge before reheating. It reheats best in a saucepan over low heat—you may need to add some additional stock or water (¼ to ½ cup) when reheating.

SHEET-PAN CILANTRO-LIME CHICKEN

SERVES 4 | TIME: 40 MINUTES

This sheet-pan chicken is one of my favorite recipes to make because it's insanely versatile. Once it's cooked, you can slice or cube the chicken and serve it in burrito bowls, you can shred it and use it for tacos or sandwiches or even pizza. Or you can serve it as is with a side of rice and beans or even chop it for a salad.

The flavors are fantastic and it will become a staple for your weeknight meals!

⅔ cup fresh cilantro, chopped, plus more for serving

½ cup extra-virgin olive oil

2 tablespoons freshly grated lime zest

¼ cup freshly squeezed lime juice

2 garlic cloves, minced

½ teaspoon crushed red pepper flakes

1 teaspoon kosher salt

1 teaspoon black pepper

1 pound boneless, skinless chicken breasts (or a mix of breasts and thighs)

½ teaspoon garlic powder

2 bell peppers, thinly sliced

1 red onion, thinly sliced

½ cup corn kernels (fresh, canned, or frozen)

3 tablespoons crumbled cotija cheese, for serving

2 tablespoons sliced jalapeño peppers, for serving

Preheat the oven to 425°F.

In a bowl, whisk together the cilantro, olive oil, lime zest and juice, garlic, red pepper flakes, and ½ teaspoon each of salt and pepper.

Season the chicken well with the remaining ½ teaspoon of salt and pepper and the garlic powder. Place the chicken on a sheet pan and surround it with the sliced bell peppers and onion. Drizzle on half of the cilantro-lime mixture and toss everything well—you want it all covered. Sprinkle the corn all over the sheet pan.

Roast for 20 to 25 minutes, or until the chicken is cooked through. Use a cooking thermometer to test the internal temperature, which should be 165°F. If at any time the peppers and onion look like they may burn, you can pull out the sheet pan and toss the veggies with a fork.

Let the chicken cool for 5 to 10 minutes before slicing or shredding. Top with more of the cilantro-lime sauce, fresh cilantro, cotija cheese, and jalapeños.

10-MINUTE MEAL PREP

- Prep the cilantro-lime mixture the night before and store it in the fridge.

- Slice your peppers and onion and store them in a sealed container in the fridge.

CHICKEN THIGHS
with creamy mustard pan sauce

SERVES 2 TO 4 | TIME: 25 MINUTES

This pan-seared chicken with creamy mustard sauce is part of my regular repertoire, one I fall back on when I can't think of something else. It is so ridiculously easy—everything is made in one pan!—but looks and tastes a bit fancier than it is.

My favorite time to make this is when we have some leftover side dish ingredients, perhaps roasted vegetables or couscous. Making this dish brings new life to the whole meal and feels extra special, even though it doesn't take any time.

And everything tastes better with a pan sauce. Trust me on that.

1 pound boneless, skinless chicken thighs

½ teaspoon garlic powder

Kosher salt and black pepper

1 tablespoon extra-virgin olive oil

2 tablespoons unsalted butter

2 garlic cloves, minced

1 small shallot, diced

⅓ cup dry white wine

1 tablespoon Dijon mustard

¼ cup heavy cream

3 tablespoons chopped fresh parsley

Pat the chicken thighs dry with a paper towel. Season them with the garlic powder and 1 teaspoon each of salt and pepper.

Add the oil to a large nonstick or cast-iron skillet over medium heat. Once the oil is hot, place the chicken in the skillet and cook for 6 minutes, then flip and cook for 4 minutes more. You want the internal temperature of the chicken to be 165°F. Transfer the chicken to a plate.

Add 1 tablespoon of the butter to the same skillet. Once it's melted, stir in the garlic and shallot. Cook, stirring often, until the shallot softens, about 5 minutes. Stir in the white wine, bring the mixture to a simmer, and cook for 5 minutes. Whisk in the mustard. Whisk in the remaining tablespoon of butter. Whisk in the cream and turn off the heat. Stir in the parsley and taste the sauce—if needed add another pinch of salt and pepper.

10-MINUTE MEAL PREP

❶ This meal comes together fairly easily, but you can dice your shallot and mince your garlic and store them together in the fridge until ready to use.

LEMON BUTTER CHICKEN

SERVES 4 | TIME: 30 MINUTES

It's here! This is easily my most-made recipe of the last ten years. It's Eddie's favorite. It's a classic. You can serve it with basically anything and the meal will be wonderful.

The chicken is tender; the sauce is lemony and rich, but somehow also light at the same time.

The method is one that my mom uses on nearly every dish she makes with chicken breasts. Cut them in half, pound them out, season and dredge, pan-fry. It's simple but the lemon butter sauce that you pour on top absolutely makes the dish!

4 boneless, skinless chicken breasts, sliced in half lengthwise

Kosher salt and freshly cracked black pepper

2 to 3 tablespoons extra-virgin olive oil

¾ cup all-purpose flour

4 tablespoons unsalted butter

2 garlic cloves, minced

1 lemon, thinly sliced

¼ cup freshly squeezed lemon juice

Chopped fresh parsley, for serving

Preheat the oven to 350°F.

Pound the chicken breasts with a meat tenderizer until they are the same thickness. Season them on both sides with 1 teaspoon each of salt and pepper.

Heat a large skillet over medium heat. Add 1 tablespoon of olive oil to the pan.

Take each chicken breast and dredge it through the flour, making sure it's completely covered but shaking off any excess. Place it in the pan and repeat with the other chicken breasts, cooking for 3 to 4 minutes, then flip and cook them for 3 minutes more. This will have to be done in batches. Transfer the chicken to a baking dish and repeat with any remaining chicken, using the remaining olive oil as necessary.

Once the chicken is out of the pan, keep the skillet over medium-low heat and add the butter. Add the garlic and cook for 30 seconds. Add the lemon slices and lemon juice. Cook for 2 to 3 minutes, flipping the lemons in the pan. Add a pinch of salt and pepper. Pour the lemon-butter mixture over the chicken in the baking dish.

Bake for 15 to 20 minutes, or until the internal temperature of the chicken reaches 165°F. Remove the chicken from the oven and sprinkle with fresh parsley. Serve immediately.

10-MINUTE MEAL PREP

❶ You can pound the chicken ahead of time and keep it stored in the fridge until ready to go.

SHEET-PAN CASHEW CHICKEN

SERVES 2 TO 4 | TIME: 35 MINUTES

There aren't many sheet-pan meals that I'm a fan of, mostly because meat and vegetables have different cooking times. It's often impossible to throw everything on a sheet pan at once and have each ingredient come out perfect.

But! I've remedied that situation for this cashew chicken. I like to roast the vegetables first, so they get caramelized and soft. THEN I add in the chicken and let it cook, tossing everything together once it's done.

The result is a saucy pan of chicken and vegetables. It's incredible on its own or perfect served over rice!

½ cup soy sauce

6 tablespoons honey

2 tablespoons rice wine vinegar

2 tablespoons toasted sesame oil

3 garlic cloves, minced

2 teaspoons freshly grated ginger

1 red bell pepper, chopped

1 orange bell pepper, chopped

1 red onion, chopped

2 boneless, skinless chicken breasts, cut into 1-inch pieces

1 cup raw unsalted cashews

Cooked brown or white rice, for serving

Chopped fresh scallions or chives, for topping

Toasted sesame seeds, for topping

Preheat the oven to 425°F.

In a bowl, whisk together the soy sauce, honey, vinegar, sesame oil, garlic, and ginger.

Place the bell peppers and onion on a baking sheet and cover them with half of the sauce. Toss well. Roast in the oven for 15 minutes. Meanwhile, place the chicken in a bowl and cover it with the remaining sauce.

After 15 minutes, push all the vegetables to one side. Place the chicken pieces in the marinade on the baking sheet. Add the cashews as well. Roast for 12 to 15 minutes, until the chicken is cooked through.

Toss everything together on the sheet before serving. Serve over rice and sprinkle with scallions and sesame seeds.

10-MINUTE MEAL PREP

❶ Make the sauce ahead of time and store it in the fridge.

❷ Chop the vegetables and the chicken and store separately in sealed containers in the fridge.

❸ You can cook the rice the day before and keep it in the fridge.

NOTE

Leftovers are wonderful and stay great in the fridge for 2 to 3 days.

NOT-SO-SLOPPY TURKEY JOES

SERVES 4 | TIME: 40 MINUTES

Welcome to another one of the most-made dinners in my kitchen. Of all time!

So, here's the crazy thing: We NEVER ate sloppy joes growing up. Not from the can, not from scratch. I'm not sure why, other than it just wasn't something my mom made. Because of that, I had it in my head for years that I didn't care for sloppy joes.

Then I watched Rachael Ray make them from scratch one day when I was home from work, sick on the couch. My mind was blown and they looked SO good. Eddie could not have been more thrilled when I made them from scratch. Turns out that it has always been one of his favorite meals.

A few rules for my sloppy joes:

I almost always use ground turkey, but you can absolutely use ground beef. I like to stir in ½ cup of lentils for an extra boost of protein and fiber. You can use all lentils, too, for a vegetarian joe!

My joes are not super sloppy. I prefer them to be perfectly sauced, but not overly sloppy, so I keep the sauciness to a minimum.

When topped with bread-and-butter pickles, these are an absolute flavor explosion. One we just can't resist.

2 tablespoons extra-virgin olive oil

1 red bell pepper, diced

1 sweet onion, diced

2 garlic cloves, minced

1 pound ground turkey (I use 94% lean)

Kosher salt and black pepper

2 tablespoons tomato paste

1 tablespoon smoked paprika

2 tablespoons brown sugar, plus more as needed

1 (15-ounce) can tomato sauce

2 teaspoons Worcestershire sauce

1 tablespoon apple cider vinegar, plus more as needed

½ cup prepared lentils (optional)

4 buttered buns, for serving

Bread-and-butter pickles, for serving

Homemade Ranch (page 54)

Heat a large skillet over medium-low heat and add the olive oil. Stir in the bell pepper, onion, and garlic. Cook until the onion softens, about 5 to 6 minutes.

Increase the heat to medium and add in the turkey with ¼ teaspoon each of salt and black pepper, using a wooden spoon to break the turkey apart and combine it with the veggies. Cook until browned. Stir in the tomato paste, smoked paprika, and brown sugar. Stir in the tomato sauce, Worcestershire, and apple cider vinegar. Stir in the lentils, if you're using them.

Cover and cook for 15 to 20 minutes, stirring often. Taste and adjust to your preferences—more salt or black pepper, more sugar if it's too tangy, more vinegar if it's too sweet.

To serve, spoon the mixture on buns or toast and top with bread-and-butter pickles. Drizzle with the homemade ranch.

10-MINUTE MEAL PREP

❶ You can make this entire dish ahead of time. The meat becomes even more flavorful as it sits in the fridge for a day or two. The best way to reheat it is in a saucepan over low heat. If needed, add ¼ cup of water or stock to reheat.

NOTE

This freezes wonderfully. Cool completely, then freeze in a sealed container for up to 3 months.

HONEY DIJON CHICKEN TENDERS
with gorgonzola

SERVES 2 TO 4 | TIME: 25 MINUTES

If you haven't figured it out by now, I really, really love anything honey Dijon. Give me alllll the mustard in the world, please!

These chicken tenders are a crowd pleaser and a kid pleaser, too. They are like sticky chicken fingers, covered in a sprinkling of tangy cheese. The honey and mustard caramelize in the skillet, turning these into delicious savory, sweet bites.

Oh, and you can always sprinkle a different cheese on top if desired.

I love to eat these as is, but leftovers are wonderful on a salad. This is my favorite chicken recipe to use for leftovers, and because of that, I often make a double batch.

2 tablespoons unsalted butter

1 pound boneless, skinless chicken tenders

½ teaspoon kosher salt

½ teaspoon freshly cracked black pepper

½ teaspoon garlic powder

3 tablespoons honey

3 tablespoons Dijon mustard

2 tablespoons chopped fresh chives

3 tablespoons crumbled Gorgonzola cheese

Heat a large nonstick skillet over medium heat and add the butter.

Season the chicken with the salt, pepper, and garlic powder. Place the chicken in the skillet and cook for 2 to 3 minutes, until golden on one side. Whisk together the honey and Dijon.

Flip the chicken and drizzle with a few spoonfuls of the honey Dijon. Cook for another 2 to 3 minutes. Flip again and drizzle with the honey Dijon. You want it to get a little caramelly in the skillet. Turn off the heat and cover with the chives and gorgonzola. Serve immediately!

SESAME-CRUSTED CHICKEN FINGERS

SERVES 4 | TIME: 35 MINUTES

Homemade chicken fingers are my family's love language. We make them for wraps, sandwiches, for dipping in sauce with a side of fries, or chopped up on salads. This sesame version is out of this world!

Avocado oil spray or olive oil spray

1 pound chicken tenders

Kosher salt and black pepper

2 large eggs

¾ cup sesame seeds

¼ cup seasoned panko bread crumbs

1 teaspoon dried chives

½ teaspoon garlic powder

Preheat the oven to 450°F. Line a baking sheet with foil and place a wire rack on top. Spray the rack with avocado oil spray.

Season the chicken tenders with salt and pepper. In one bowl, lightly beat the eggs. In a second bowl, stir together the sesame seeds, bread crumbs, chives, and garlic powder until combined.

Take a chicken tender and coat it in the beaten egg. Dredge it through the sesame mixture, pressing gently so the crumbs adhere. Place the tender on the prepared rack and repeat with the remaining chicken. Once all the chicken is finished, spray it with avocado oil spray. This helps the chicken crisp up!

Bake the chicken for 12 minutes. Flip it gently and spray the other side with the oil spray. Bake for another 10 to 12 minutes.

Cool slightly before serving.

10-MINUTE MEAL PREP

- Stir together the sesame and bread crumb mixture and store it in the pantry until ready to use.

CHICKEN AND BACON RANCH PUFF PASTRY PIZZA

SERVES 2 TO 4 | TIME: 35 MINUTES

Puff pastry is a miracle worker. I keep some in my freezer at all times—it's fabulous for pot pies, quick biscuits, desserts, and especially pizza.

Our favorite local pizza is made with a pastry-like crust, and the puff pastry replicates it almost exactly. It's wonderful! So wonderful, in fact, that I've created four puff pastry pizzas for you in this book, way beyond pepperoni and cheese. Be sure to also check out Zucchini, Lemon, and Goat Cheese Puff Pastry Pizza (page 115); Mushroom, Fontina, and Balsamic Puff Pastry Pizza (page 116); and Prosciutto, Pesto, and Pistachio Puff Pastry Pizza (page 193)!

This one is an ode to one of my favorite childhood sandwiches. The combination is great—crunchy from the bacon, rich from the cheese, fresh from the herbs, and oh-so satisfying.

3 slices bacon, chopped

1 sheet frozen puff pastry, thawed

½ cup ranch dressing

½ teaspoon dried dill

½ teaspoon dried chives

⅔ cup cooked and shredded chicken

¾ cup freshly grated Cheddar cheese

2 scallions, thinly sliced

2 tablespoons chopped fresh dill

Preheat the oven to 425°F. Line a baking sheet with parchment paper.

Heat a large skillet over medium heat. Add the bacon and cook until it just begins to crisp. Do not cook all the way or it will burn in the oven! Scoop the bacon out with a slotted spoon and place it on a paper towel to remove excess grease.

Place the sheet of puff pastry on the prepared baking sheet. Spread ⅓ cup of the ranch dressing on the puff pastry, leaving a 1-inch border on the edges. Sprinkle the dried dill and chives along the edges. Scatter the chicken and cheese over the ranch dressing. Sprinkle the bacon on top.

Bake for 20 to 25 minutes, or until golden and crisp. Remove from the oven and drizzle with the remaining ranch and sprinkle with the scallions and fresh dill. Puff pastry is best served shortly after making.

10-MINUTE MEAL PREP

- Cook the bacon ahead of time and store it in the fridge. You can also use rotisserie chicken.

- Grate the cheese and store it in the fridge.

- Make sure to thaw the puff pastry sheet.

PORK

So, here's the deal: I could probably live as a vegetarian if it weren't for pork!

Many of my favorite dishes include bacon, prosciutto, and pulled pork—I know, shocking, right? I mean, they're all extra delicious. And while I don't use them every night, one dish that I find to be underutilized during the week is pork tenderloin. It cooks more quickly than expected, but so many people are intimidated by it. You'll find an incredible recipe for that in this section, along with another sheet-pan gnocchi and a puff pastry pizza—two of my go-tos.

I've rounded out the chapter with salads and chops so you're good to go.

BLT CORN SALAD

SERVES 4 | TIME: 15 MINUTES

If you need a corn salad that pleases everyone, you've got it. Sweet corn, crunchy bacon, ripe tomatoes, peppery arugula, and fresh basil ribbons—this is everything you want in a bite. Serve with all of your favorite summer dishes! Use it as a salsa or stir it into pasta or rice.

4 slices of bacon, chopped

6 ears of sweet corn, kernels cut from the cob

2 cups fresh arugula

1 cup cherry tomatoes, diced

¼ cup chopped fresh basil

Pinch of kosher salt and black pepper

Heat a large skillet over medium heat and add the bacon. Cook, tossing occasionally, until the bacon is crispy and the fat is rendered. Remove the bacon with a slotted spoon and place it on a paper towel to drain any excess grease.

In a large bowl, toss the corn with the arugula, diced cherry tomatoes, and basil. Add salt and pepper and stir.

Stir in the bacon. Serve!

10-MINUTE MEAL PREP

- Cook the bacon ahead of time and store it in the fridge.

- Cut the kernels from the cob ahead of time and store them in the fridge.

- Chop the tomatoes ahead of time and store them in the fridge.

HONEY MUSTARD CHICKPEA COBB SALAD

SERVES 2 TO 4 | TIME: 30 MINUTES

Cobb salads were one of the first salads I ever truly enjoyed, and, yes, I'm sure that's because of the bacon, cheese, and eggs. And the fact that everything is chopped and in perfect bite-size pieces, just waiting for a fork grab.

I've never stopped enjoying the idea of a Cobb salad with all its chopped ingredients, but I have taken matters into my own hands to create a version that I really adore. First, enter chickpeas. I'd rather have these over chicken any day, and I usually have them on hand.

I keep the bacon and the eggs, because they are vital to the salad. Plus, hello FLAVOR.

I like to do blue cheese, because it's my favorite, but you can use cubed white Cheddar or feta instead. I also love avocado for the creamy, satisfying bite.

This salad uses what is perhaps my favorite dressing of all time: honey mustard vinaigrette. It's so flavorful and tangy without being overly creamy.

Toss it all together or eat it bite by bite. It's perfect in every way!

3 large eggs

4 slices bacon

1 (14-ounce) can chickpeas, drained and rinsed

1 cup cherry tomatoes, chopped

½ cup chopped cucumber

1 avocado, cubed

¼ cup crumbled blue cheese

Honey Mustard Vinaigrette (page 57)

3 tablespoons chopped fresh herbs, like chives and basil

Place the eggs in a pot and cover with cold water. Bring the water to a boil over medium heat and boil for 1 minute. Turn off the heat and cover the pot. Let it sit for 10 minutes, then drop the eggs into an ice bath. Once cool, peel and slice the eggs.

While the eggs cook, heat a skillet over medium-low heat. Add the bacon and cook until crisp and crunchy. Remove it and place it on a paper towel to drain any excess grease. Once cool, crumble the bacon.

To assemble the salad, place the chickpeas, tomatoes, cucumber, avocado, and cheese in segments on the plate. Add in the bacon and the eggs. Drizzle with the honey mustard vinaigrette and top with the fresh herbs.

10-MINUTE MEAL PREP

- Make the eggs a day or two before and store them in the fridge.
- Cook the bacon ahead of time and store it in the fridge.
- Make the dressing a day or two before and store it in the fridge.

STICKY, SAUCY GRILLED PORK TENDERLOIN with chipotle corn salad

SERVES 4 | TIME: 45 MINUTES

In my opinion, pork tenderloin is such an underrated weeknight dish. It's full of flavor, serves many, and also cooks more quickly than you'd think—in about 25 minutes or so.

This one is saucy and sticky and grilled to perfection, with crispy, charred bits on the outside when it's all done. The best part of this meal, however, is the chipotle corn salad. I basically want to use it as a base for absolutely EVERYTHING these days. It's creamy and sweet, with a hint of heat. Use fresh sweet corn, grilled corn, or frozen corn that's been steamed. Fresh herbs bring this dish to life. It will truly become one of your favorites!

3 tablespoons honey

3 tablespoons soy sauce

1 tablespoon brown sugar

2 garlic cloves, minced

Kosher salt and black pepper

1 (2-pound) pork tenderloin

Chipotle Corn Salad (recipe follows)

Preheat your grill to medium-high heat—ideally we want the temperature to be around 500°F. Let the grill heat for at least 15 minutes. While the grill heats up, you can marinate the pork and start working on the corn salad.

In a bowl, whisk together the honey, soy sauce, brown sugar, and garlic with a pinch of salt and pepper. Marinate the pork in the sauce, even if it's just for 15 minutes.

To grill the pork, remove the tenderloin from the marinade, allowing the marinade to drip off as much as it can. Place the tenderloin on the grill. You want to cook it for 20 to 25 minutes total. I flip it after 8 minutes, then turn it again after another 8 minutes. You want the inside temperature to be 140–145°F. Make sure to go by what the thermometer says, because the heat on every grill can differ!

Once the tenderloin is finished, place it on a sheet pan or dish and let it rest for 15 minutes. Then slice and serve with the chipotle corn salad.

10-MINUTE MEAL PREP

❷ Mix together the sauce and marinate the pork overnight if you wish.

❷ The corn salad can be fully prepared a few hours ahead or the night before serving.

chipotle corn salad

6 ears of corn, kernels cut from the cob

2 scallions, thinly sliced

1 avocado, diced

¼ cup chopped fresh cilantro

¼ cup sour cream

1 chipotle pepper (from a can), diced

1 tablespoon adobo sauce from the can of chipotles

Juice of 1 lime

Pinch of kosher salt and black pepper

In a bowl, combine the corn, scallions, avocado, and cilantro.

In a smaller bowl, whisk together the sour cream, chipotle pepper, adobo sauce, lime juice, and salt and pepper. Stir the sour cream mixture into the corn until combined. Serve immediately with the pork.

SHEET-PAN GNOCCHI FOR WINTER

Winter
Brussels Sprouts and Pancetta

SERVES 2 AS A MEAL, 4 AS A SIDE DISH | TIME: 35 MINUTES

In 2018, I fell in love with throwing gnocchi on a sheet pan and roasting it in the oven with vegetables. The end result is a crisp, golden gnocchi—but one that is still pillowy and cloud-like in the center when you take a bite.

After everything roasts on a sheet pan, you can toss it together and serve it. I've loved the classic version so much, which is just gnocchi, peppers, onions, and tomatoes, that I've created this and three more flavors of sheet-pan gnocchi to work with seasonal ingredients (page 107).

Nonstick cooking spray

4 ounces diced pancetta

1 (16-ounce) package uncooked potato gnocchi

1½ cups Brussels sprouts, stems removed and quartered

3 tablespoons extra-virgin olive oil

1 teaspoon garlic powder

1 teaspoon kosher salt

½ teaspoon freshly cracked black pepper

3 tablespoons heavy cream

¼ cup freshly shaved Parmesan cheese, for topping

Pinch of crushed red pepper flakes

Sprinkle of chopped fresh herbs, like parsley, if desired

Preheat your oven to 425°F. Spray a baking sheet with nonstick spray.

Heat a nonstick skillet over medium heat. Place the pancetta in the skillet and cook slightly, just until some of the fat is rendered, about 2 minutes or so. You don't want to crisp up the pancetta too much because it will burn in the oven! Remove the pancetta with a slotted spoon and place it on a paper towel to drain any excess grease.

Spread the gnocchi and Brussels sprouts out on the prepared baking sheet in a single layer. Drizzle with the olive oil and toss. Sprinkle with the pancetta, garlic powder, salt, and black pepper. Toss well to combine. Make sure everything is seasoned well!

Roast for 20 to 25 minutes, tossing once during cook time.

Serve the gnocchi immediately. Drizzle with the cream. Sprinkle with the Parmesan, red pepper flakes, and a sprinkling of fresh herbs, if using. Toss well and serve.

10-MINUTE MEAL PREP

- Parcook the pancetta ahead of time and store it in the fridge.

- Quarter the Brussels sprouts ahead of time and store in the fridge.

GRILLED PEACH BBQ PORK CHOPS
with napa slaw

SERVES 4 | TIME: 40 MINUTES

The best secret to grilling good pork chops? Brine them first! This has changed the way I make pork chops: it keeps them moist and juicy.

I love to make these on the grill with my peach BBQ sauce. They are smoky and sweet and tender. Serve atop my favorite slaw made with lime and toasted sesame oil. It's crunchy and delicious!

¼ cup kosher salt

4 bone-in pork chops

1 teaspoon freshly cracked black pepper

1 teaspoon garlic powder

2 peaches, halved and pitted

½ cup Peach BBQ sauce (page 47)

Napa Slaw (recipe follows)

To make the brine, combine 6 cups of water with the kosher salt in a large bowl, stirring together until the salt dissolves. You can also heat the mixture to dissolve the salt and let it cool completely. Place the pork chops in a baking dish and pour the brine over them. I brine mine for just 20 to 30 minutes.

Meanwhile, heat the grill to the highest setting and let it heat for 10 minutes.

Remove the pork chops from the brine and pat them dry completely with paper towels. Sprinkle them with the pepper and garlic powder.

Once the grill is hot, add the pork chops and cook for 6 minutes. You can also add the peaches at this time if you'd like—they only need about 5 minutes total on the grill. Flip the chops, and brush the top side with the BBQ sauce. Cook for 6 minutes more. Flip again and brush the other side with the sauce. Continue to grill, about 8 to 10 minutes more, flipping every few minutes and brushing with the sauce, until the internal temperature reaches 145°F.

Let rest for a few minutes before serving with more of the sauce and the napa slaw.

10-MINUTE MEAL PREP

- Make the BBQ sauce ahead of time and store in the fridge.
- Brine the pork chops for up to a few hours ahead of time.
- Prep the slaw 1 hour ahead.

napa slaw

3 cups shredded napa cabbage

1 red bell pepper, thinly sliced

½ red onion, thinly sliced

1 jalapeño pepper, seeded and thinly sliced

2 tablespoons toasted sesame oil

2 tablespoons freshly squeezed lime juice

Kosher salt and black pepper, to taste

In a large bowl, toss together the cabbage, bell pepper, onion, jalapeño, sesame oil, lime juice, and salt and black pepper so everything is combined and covered in the sesame and lime. This stays great in the fridge for 1 day.

PROSCIUTTO, PESTO, PISTACHIO PUFF PASTRY PIZZA

SERVES 2 TO 4 | TIME: 35 MINUTES

Another day, another puff pastry pizza. I can't help myself—this is the easiest way to throw a pizza together in 25 minutes at home. And it's better than a tortilla or pita for a base. Flaky layers with lots of pesto, crisp prosciutto, and pistachios. Sign me up.

1 sheet frozen puff pastry, thawed

⅓ cup Classic Pesto (page 42)

4 ounces thinly sliced prosciutto, torn into pieces

1 (8-ounce) ball fresh mozzarella, thinly sliced

¼ cup chopped pistachios

Preheat the oven to 425°F. Line a baking sheet with parchment paper.

Place the sheet of puff pastry on the prepared baking sheet. Spread the pesto on the pastry, leaving a 1-inch border. Top with the prosciutto and cheese. Cover with the pistachios.

Bake for 20 to 25 minutes, or until golden and crisp. Slice and serve.

10-MINUTE MEAL PREP

- Make the pesto ahead of time and store it in the fridge.
- Chop the pistachios ahead of time and store in the pantry.

ONE-POT SAUSAGE, GREENS, AND BEANS PASTA

SERVES 4 | TIME: 40 MINUTES

I live for a meal where you can simply add all the ingredients to one pot and be rewarded with something delicious.

In this dish, we're making absolutely everything in one pot, covering it with some water, and letting it cook until a creamy, dreamy pasta results. It's flavorful and spicy and buttery from the beans. It's satisfying (because hi, pasta) and savory thanks to the cheese.

Top it with a sprinkle of crushed red pepper flakes for extra heat. And, of course, Parmesan shavings, because I can't live without them.

2 teaspoons extra-virgin olive oil

½ pound Italian sausage

1 shallot, diced

4 garlic cloves, minced

Kosher salt

1 bunch of Swiss chard, leaves removed from stems and torn

8 ounces whole-wheat gemelli pasta, or a similar shape

3½ cups low-sodium vegetable or chicken stock

½ teaspoon black pepper

½ cup freshly grated Parmesan cheese, plus more if desired

1 (14-ounce) can white beans, drained and rinsed

Pinch of crushed red pepper flakes, for topping

Heat a large pot over medium heat and add the olive oil. Add the sausage and break it apart with a wooden spoon, crumbling it as much as you can. Cook until browned, about 6 to 8 minutes. Remove the sausage with a slotted spoon and transfer it to a plate.

Keep the same pot over medium-low heat and add the shallot and garlic with a pinch of salt. Cook for 5 minutes, then stir in the torn Swiss chard. Cook for 5 minutes more. Add in the pasta, stock, 1 teaspoon salt, and the black pepper.

Bring the mixture to a boil and then cook for 8 to 10 minutes, stirring often, so the pasta cooks. Once the noodles have absorbed all of the water, remove the pot from the heat. Stir in the Parmesan, the cooked sausage, and the beans. Cook for 5 to 10 more minutes, until everything is warm and the cheese is melty.

Serve immediately, adding the red pepper flakes and more Parmesan on top, if desired.

10-MINUTE MEAL PREP

- You can brown the sausage ahead of time and store it in the fridge.

- Wash and tear the Swiss chard ahead of time and store it in the fridge.

ASPARAGUS BUNDLES
with soft-boiled eggs and dijon drizzle

SERVES 2 | TIME: 30 MINUTES

The classic asparagus-plus-egg combo is one that I love so much. I do agree with the adage that everything is better with an egg, and this asparagus is no exception.

Roasting asparagus is my favorite way to prepare it, so you can imagine how delicious it is when you wrap bundles of it in thinly sliced prosciutto.

The asparagus becomes crunchy and the prosciutto slices crisp up like bacon. The soft-boiled eggs add a wonderful richness. Of course, you can just poach or fry eggs instead—whichever you prefer.

A quick Dijon honey drizzled on at the end really takes things over the top and makes this meal extra special.

4 large eggs

1 pound asparagus spears, woody stems removed

4 slices prosciutto

2 teaspoons extra-virgin olive oil

¼ teaspoon freshly cracked black pepper

3 tablespoons Dijon mustard

3 tablespoons honey

Preheat the oven to 425°F.

To soft-boil the eggs: In a small saucepan, heat about 3 inches of water over medium heat until boiling. Once boiling, reduce the heat until it's barely at a simmer, add the eggs gently, and cook for 6 minutes. Remove the eggs with a slotted spoon and place in an ice bath. Let cool completely before peeling.

Group the asparagus spears into four bundles. This depends on how many spears you have—if you have 20 spears, each bundle will have 5 pieces!

Wrap the prosciutto around the asparagus, creating the bundle. Place the bundles on a baking sheet and drizzle with olive oil, then sprinkle with pepper. Roast for 15 to 18 minutes, or until the prosciutto is just crispy.

Whisk together the Dijon and the honey.

Serve the asparagus with the eggs on top and the Dijon honey drizzled over.

10-MINUTE MEAL PREP

- Soft-boil the eggs a few hours before.
- Trim the ends from the asparagus and store the spears in the fridge.
- Wrap the asparagus in prosciutto and store in the fridge until ready to roast.

CHIPOTLE BACON AND BLUE CHEESE DUTCH BABY

SERVES 4 | TIME: 30 MINUTES

I didn't grow up in a house that served a Dutch baby—a large, fluffy, baked pancake—and I'm so jealous of those who did. Not only is a Dutch baby delicious, it also feeds a crowd and is pretty darn easy. The ingredients are thrown in a blender, then poured in a pan and baked! Super simple!

I have extra love for this Dutch baby because it's a savory version. Fresh chives are used to make the savory pancake and the entire thing is topped with spicy bacon and creamy blue cheese. It's divine.

3 tablespoons unsalted butter

3 eggs

1 cup all-purpose flour

1 cup milk, warmed

3 tablespoons chives, plus more for serving

¼ teaspoon kosher salt

8 slices thick-cut bacon, chopped

2 teaspoons brown sugar

½ teaspoon chipotle chile powder

½ cup crumbled blue cheese

1 cup microgreens

Preheat the oven to 400°F.

Put the butter in a large, ovenproof, nonstick 10-inch pan and place in the oven until the butter melts.

Meanwhile, in a blender, combine the eggs, flour, warm milk, chives, and salt, and blend on medium-high speed until smooth.

Carefully remove the hot pan from the oven. The butter should be melted. Brush the butter around the pan to coat completely, and then pour the remaining butter into the batter and pulse to blend. Pour the batter into the hot pan and return the pan to the oven. Cook until the Dutch baby is puffed in the center and golden brown along the edges, 20 to 25 minutes.

While the Dutch baby bakes, make the bacon. Heat a skillet over medium heat and add the bacon. Cook just until the fat has rendered and the bacon is not quite crispy. In a bowl, whisk together the sugar and chile powder. Sprinkle it over the bacon and toss and stir. Cook until the bacon is fully crispy, then remove it with a slotted spoon and place on a paper towel to drain excess grease.

Using a spatula, remove the entire Dutch baby from the pan and place on a cooling rack for 1 to 2 minutes to allow the steam to escape without soaking the bottom.

Top the Dutch baby with the chipotle bacon and blue cheese while it's still warm. Sprinkle on the microgreens and some extra chives. Slice and serve immediately.

BEEF

Beef makes an appearance at our dinner table every other week or so. We don't eat a lot of red meat, but Eddie loves a good steak and some of our all-time weeknight faves include ground beef or flank steak.

When it comes to ground beef, I often swap it out for ground turkey. Sometimes even ground chicken. I also like to mix the two together. Feel free to do the same here.

TACO SALAD IN A JAR

SERVES 1 TO 2 | TIME: 30 MINUTES

In my opinion, salads in a jar are one of the BEST meals to prep ahead of time. There is nothing better than realizing come mealtime that you have a loaded salad with your favorite ingredients prepped and ready—with dressing and all!

Here's the secret: The key is in the layering. All sauces should go on the bottom, followed by heavier ingredients. Looser and lighter ingredients go on top, of course. You can mix everything up in the jar and eat it as so, or you can dump it out into a bowl and toss it all together. This is another recipe where it's important to add what YOU love in a taco salad. (Or what you may have on hand!)

It's great to make with leftover ingredients after you have tacos for dinner. It's a fabulous clean-out-the-fridge meal at the end of the week, too.

Below I'm sharing some loose measurements of how to throw your jar salad together, but keep in mind that there is no real recipe. Add the ingredients that you love the most. Use taco meat or keep it meat-free and go with extra beans. Make it your own!

2 tablespoons plain Greek yogurt

2 tablespoons Quick and Easy Guacamole (page 39)

2 tablespoons Taco Sauce (page 38)

¼ cup pinto beans

¼ cup Our Favorite Taco Meat (page 205)

¼ cup fresh or cooked sweet corn kernels

¼ cup Quick Pico de Gallo (page 39)

¼ cup freshly grated white Cheddar cheese

1 cup shredded lettuce

1 handful fresh cilantro , chopped

Lime wedges, for spritzing

Tortilla chips, for topping!

In a jar, start with layers of the yogurt, guac, and taco sauce at the bottom. Add layers of the beans, taco meat, corn, pico, and Cheddar. Add the lettuce and cilantro at the very top, and cover the jar. This stays great in the fridge for 24 hours. When ready to serve, dump the ingredients into a bowl, using a spoon or spatula to scrape the guac and yogurt from the bottom. Toss the salad well and spritz with fresh lime.

Crush tortilla chips on top and serve.

10-MINUTE MEAL PREP

❶ This entire recipe can be prepped ahead of time.

❷ To prep parts of the recipe before assembly, make the taco meat, the pico, the guacamole, and the taco sauce ahead of time. All of them stay great in the fridge for a few days!

OUR FAVORITE TACO MEAT

SERVES 4 | TIME: 25 MINUTES

I grew up in a house that had taco night every week. And by taco night, I mean skillet-crumbled, packet-seasoned ground beef, served in hard shells with cheese, tomatoes, sour cream, and lettuce.

It's easy to say that a meal like that weekly fed my taco obsession. The only thing I didn't love was the cumin-heavy spice packet. I was always determined to make my own version of taco meat with pantry spices, and this is the absolute best.

This is one of my go-to freezer recipes, too. Once cooled, you can place this in a sealed container and freeze it for up to 3 months. It was wonderful to have on hand after I had babies, because I used it for tacos, stuffed peppers, enchiladas, nachos, and salads. It's also a great one to give away as a freezer meal!

Oh! Of course you can use ground turkey here. Even ground chicken! I often mix one pound of ground beef and one pound of ground turkey, and then double the spice. It's a great recipe to experiment with.

1 tablespoon extra-virgin olive oil

1 bell pepper, diced

1 shallot, diced

2 garlic cloves, minced

Kosher salt

1 pound lean ground beef
(I like 94% lean)

2 teaspoons ground cumin

2 teaspoons smoked paprika

1 teaspoon chili powder

½ teaspoon garlic powder

½ teaspoon freshly cracked black pepper

1 teaspoon all-purpose flour

Heat a large skillet over medium heat and add the olive oil. Add the bell pepper, shallot, and garlic with a pinch of salt. Cook, stirring often, until softened, about 5 minutes.

Add in the ground beef, breaking it apart with a wooden spoon. Add the cumin, smoked paprika, chili powder, garlic powder, ½ teaspoon of salt, and the black pepper. Stir well, continuing to break apart the meat into small crumbles. Cook until the beef has browned.

In a jar, combine ½ cup of water and the flour and shake for 30 seconds. Pour the mixture into the meat, stirring well and cooking for another 5 to 6 minutes, until saucy. Serve as desired.

10-MINUTE MEAL PREP

- Measure out the spices and combine ahead of time.
- Chop the bell pepper, garlic, and shallot ahead of time and store in the fridge.
- This entire dish can be made ahead of time—leftovers are great!

NOTE

Freeze in a sealed container for up to 3 months. To reheat, thaw and add to a saucepan with a few tablespoons of stock or water.

SEARED STEAKHOUSE SALAD
with potatoes and greens

SERVES 2 TO 4 | TIME: 35 MINUTES

If you're craving a hearty salad, I have just the meal for you! This steakhouse salad is Eddie's dream—all steak and potatoes with a hint of greens for freshness. It's a great summer evening salad; one that usually pleases everyone.

My favorite part of this salad is the blue cheese vinaigrette. Yes! It's not a creamy blue cheese dressing, but instead a vinaigrette with marinated crumbled blue cheese that tastes absolutely wonderful. Of course, it's great on all kinds of salads. But it truly complements the steak and potato dish here. You will love it!

8 baby Yukon Gold potatoes, cut in half

2 (3- to 4-ounce) strip steaks, at room temperature for 15 minutes

Kosher salt and black pepper

2 tablespoons unsalted butter

6 to 8 cups spring greens

½ red onion, thinly sliced, or Quick Pickled Onions (page 35)

Blue Cheese Vinaigrette (page 51)

¼ cup crumbled blue cheese

Place the potatoes in a pot and cover them with cold water. Bring to a boil over medium heat and boil for 10 to 15 minutes, until fork-tender. Drain and let cool slightly.

While the potatoes boil, heat a heavy-bottomed skillet over medium-high heat. Season the steaks with salt and pepper generously all over. Melt the butter in the skillet. Add the steaks to the skillet and sear on both sides for 2 to 3 minutes per side. Turn off the heat and keep the steaks in the pan for an additional 1 to 2 minutes, spooning the butter over them. Remove the steaks and let them rest for 10 minutes, then thinly slice.

To assemble the salad, combine the greens and red onion in a bowl with a pinch of salt and pepper. Toss well, then top with the boiled potatoes and sliced steak. Drizzle all over with the blue cheese vinaigrette and top with the crumbled blue cheese. Serve immediately.

10-MINUTE MEAL PREP

- Boil the potatoes ahead of time and keep them in the fridge.

- Sear the steak ahead of time and store it in the fridge, if you don't mind eating a cold salad.

- Make the dressing ahead of time and store it in the fridge.

CHEESEBURGER SUMMER ROLLS

SERVES 2 TO 4 | TIME: 30 MINUTES

The inspiration for this meal came from my brother, after he fell in love with cheeseburger spring rolls—the fried version. The idea played into my cravings for weeks. I took matters into my own hands and made summer rolls instead, which are wrapped in rice paper and are the epitome of freshness. Even with the cheeseburger ingredients.

The rice paper wrappers have a bit of a learning curve, but once you get used to wrapping, these spring rolls are easy to make. I absolutely love this recipe because most of the ingredients stuffed inside are crispy. The lettuce is refreshing while the crumbled Cheddar beef is comforting. I like to add pickles because I can't live without them, but I encourage you to add whatever you love on a burger.

1 teaspoon extra-virgin olive oil

½ pound lean ground beef (I like 94% lean)

2 garlic cloves, minced

¼ teaspoon kosher salt

¼ teaspoon black pepper

4 ounces freshly grated sharp white Cheddar cheese

8 pieces of lettuce, Swiss chard, or another green

½ pint cherry tomatoes, halved or quartered

⅓ cup chopped dill pickles

¼ cup diced red onion

8 rice paper wrappers

Dipping Sauce (below)

Heat a large skillet over medium heat and add the olive oil. Once it's hot, add the ground beef, garlic, salt, and pepper. Break the mixture apart with a wooden spoon and cook until browned, stirring occasionally and breaking the pieces into crumbles, for about 6 to 8 minutes. Turn off the heat and sprinkle about half of the cheese over the beef so it slightly melts. Let the beef cool—almost to room temperature.

Set up an assembly line with the lettuce, beef, remaining cheese, tomatoes, pickles, and onion.

To assemble the rolls, fill a round cake pan or skillet with warm water. Dip each piece of rice paper in the water to coat it completely, then immediately remove it (don't let it sit in the water!). Place the rice paper on a cutting board and top it with a piece of the lettuce.

Top with a spoonful of beef, a sprinkling of cheese, tomatoes, pickles, and onion. Start rolling from one end and fold in the sides as you go. The paper will stick together and your roll will hold! Repeat with the remaining ingredients.

Serve with dipping sauce.

10-MINUTE MEAL PREP

- These rolls are best made shortly before eating, but you can prep and chop the ingredients ahead of time: Grate your cheese, cook your beef, and wash and chop the vegetables. Store everything in the fridge until ready to use.

- The dipping sauce can be made ahead of time and stored in the fridge.

dipping sauce

½ cup mayonnaise

¼ cup ketchup

2 teaspoons sweet pickle relish

1 teaspoon apple cider vinegar

1 teaspoon ground black pepper

In a bowl, whisk together the mayonnaise, ketchup, relish, vinegar, and pepper until combined.

FLANK STEAK
with lime chimichurri

SERVES 2 TO 4 | TIME: 35 MINUTES (PLUS HANDS-OFF TIME TO MARINATE)

When I was growing up, my dad made flank steak ALL the time. My mom would marinate it a few hours before he came home and then he would grill it. It was a meal that we all loved and one that provided leftovers for the next day, too.

This version is served with an extra lime-y chimichurri. It's fantastic served on its own or on a baguette, open faced with some greens. The chimichurri is made with loads of fresh herbs and is wonderful to make if your garden is overflowing. It also freezes beautifully so you can always have some on hand.

1 (2-pound) flank steak, about 1 inch thick

½ teaspoon kosher salt

½ teaspoon black pepper

⅓ cup extra-virgin olive oil

3 tablespoons brown sugar

4 garlic cloves, minced

Lime Chimichurri (below)

Add the flank steak to a large baking dish and season it with the salt and pepper. In a bowl, whisk together the olive oil, brown sugar, and garlic, then pour it over the steak. Place the steak in the fridge to marinate—anywhere from 30 minutes to overnight.

When you're ready to cook the steak, you can grill, broil, or pan-sear it to your liking. I tend to broil it as I find that easiest. Preheat the broiler in your oven and move the oven rack to the highest level. Place the steak on a broiler pan or baking sheet and broil on each side for about 5 minutes for medium to medium-well. The internal temp should read 155°F for medium steak.

Allow the steak to rest for 10 minutes before slicing it thinly against the grain. Serve it immediately with the chimichurri.

lime chimichurri

⅔ cup fresh parsley

1 cup fresh cilantro

2 garlic cloves, minced

2 tablespoons red wine vinegar

2 tablespoons freshly squeezed lime juice

⅔ cup extra-virgin olive oil

1 tablespoon grated lime zest

½ teaspoon kosher salt

½ teaspoon black pepper

¼ teaspoon crushed red pepper flakes

In a food processor, combine the parsley, cilantro, and garlic and pulse a few times until small leaves and pieces remain—don't puree. Add in the vinegar and lime juice and pulse once more. With the processor going, stream in the olive oil and pulse again until just combined. Stir in the lime zest, salt, black pepper, and red pepper flakes. Taste and season additionally if needed. Store in a sealed container in the fridge for 3 to 4 days or freeze and use within 3 months.

10-MINUTE MEAL PREP

❶ Marinate the steak the night before. Remove it from the fridge 30 minutes before cooking.

❷ Prepare the chimichurri and store it in the fridge.

SMOKY STUFFED POBLANOS

SERVES 4 | TIME: 35 MINUTES

I often crave a modern twist on a classic, and this recipe fits the bill. Eddie adores a classic stuffed pepper with sausage and a tomato-based sauce. But I wish for something off the beaten path, with smoky beef and avocado crema stuffed in rich, earthy poblano peppers.

This is a recipe that takes a little extra work ahead of time—both the meat and the rice have to be cooked before they are stuffed in the peppers. However, those are two quick aspects of meal prep that can be done a day or two ahead of time. If you're in a pinch on a weeknight, you can brown the ground beef and use instant rice. Use both the avocado crema and quick pico, or just pick one. Top with jarred salsa instead and your favorite guac. There are no rules when it comes to toppings, other than to use what you love.

4 poblano peppers

1 pound lean ground beef (I like 94% lean)

1 teaspoon ground cumin

1 teaspoon smoked paprika

½ teaspoon garlic powder

½ teaspoon chili powder

½ teaspoon kosher salt

½ teaspoon freshly cracked black pepper

⅔ cup beef stock

1½ cups cooked jasmine rice

Avocado Crema (page 47)

Quick Pico de Gallo (page 39), for topping

Preheat the oven to 350°F.

Slice the poblanos lengthwise and remove the seeds. Place the poblanos on a baking sheet.

Heat a skillet over medium heat and add the beef. Break it apart with a wooden spoon. Season with the cumin, smoked paprika, garlic powder, chili powder, salt, and pepper. Cook until browned, stirring and breaking pieces apart occasionally, about 6 to 8 minutes. Once it's browned, stir in the stock. This gives it some moisture so it doesn't dry out in the pepper. You can either toss the rice right into the beef at this point, or add the beef and rice to the pepper separately.

Fill the peppers with the beef and rice. Bake for 20 minutes, until everything is heated through.

While the peppers cook, blend the ingredients together for your avocado crema. You can also make the quick pico, chopping and combining everything.

When the peppers are finished, drizzle with the avocado crema and top with the pico. Serve!

10-MINUTE MEAL PREP

- This is a great meal to prep ahead—cook both the rice and beef and store them in the fridge for 2 to 3 days before making the stuffed peppers.

- The avocado crema and quick pico can be made 1 to 2 days ahead of time.

've loved any and all seafood since I was a kid—lobsters, clams, scallops, and fresh fish—there is nothing better.

My dad would catch whitefish on the shores of Lake Charlevoix in the summer, come home, and make a light beer batter before frying it up. We'd also vacation in New Jersey, where my uncle would make seafood boils on a picnic table by the pool—or even in a cooler that we would drag to the beach.

SEAFOOD

These days, we eat lots of salmon for dinner, fish tacos prepared in every way imaginable, and scallops seared in brown butter. I love how versatile seafood can be. I also love how light but satiating it is.

This section is packed with some of my favorite shrimp recipes, a pretzel-crusted salmon (OMG!), and crispy fish tacos that take me back to the shore.

ROASTED CHILI-LIME SHRIMP TACO SALAD

SERVES 2 TO 4 | TIME: 35 MINUTES

This roasted chili-lime shrimp is so flavorful and comes together quickly. While it's easy to pan-fry shrimp in a skillet, roasting has become my new favorite way of preparation because it takes little effort, aside from preheating the oven. Plus, if you have a larger family, you can make the shrimp on a big sheet pan instead of in batches.

Like many of my other favorite taco-inspired recipes, this is the space to use up ingredients in your fridge or leftovers from taco or fajita night. Make sure you season the heck out of your greens, and add the crunch or texture so many of us crave.

SHRIMP

1 pound shrimp, peeled and deveined

¼ cup extra-virgin olive oil

1 teaspoon chili powder

1 teaspoon freshly grated lime zest

Kosher salt and black pepper

SALAD

6 to 8 cups green leaf or butter lettuce, or whatever lettuce you love!

Kosher salt and black pepper

1 (14-ounce) can black beans, drained and rinsed

1 avocado, cubed

1 cup grape tomatoes, halved

½ cup fresh or cooked sweet corn kernels

⅓ cup crumbled cotija cheese

¼ cup sliced scallions

¼ cup chopped fresh cilantro

Crushed tortilla chips, for topping

CHILI-LIME DRESSING

2 tablespoons freshly squeezed lime juice

1½ tablespoons honey

2 garlic cloves, minced or pressed

¼ teaspoon chili powder

1 tablespoon chopped fresh cilantro

Kosher salt and black pepper

⅓ cup extra-virgin olive oil

To make the shrimp: Preheat the oven to 425°F. In a bowl or resealable bag, toss the shrimp with the olive oil, chili powder, lime zest, and ½ teaspoon each of salt and pepper. Let it marinate for 5 minutes.

Place the shrimp on a sheet pan and roast for 6 to 8 minutes, or until opaque and pink.

To make the salad: Place the lettuce in a large bowl and season it with a pinch of salt and pepper—this is key to a flavorful salad! Toss well.

Add the beans, avocado, tomatoes, corn, cotija cheese, scallions, and cilantro to the lettuce. Add on the shrimp however you'd like—you can top the salad with it or mix it in.

To make the dressing: In a bowl, whisk together the lime juice, honey, garlic, chili powder, cilantro, and a pinch of salt and pepper. Stream in the olive oil while whisking until the dressing is emulsified. This dressing stays great in the fridge for a few days!

Toss the salad with the chili-lime dressing. Sprinkle on crushed tortilla chips.

10-MINUTE MEAL PREP

❶ The dressing can be made ahead of time and stored in the fridge.

❷ Some of the salad ingredients—like the tomatoes and scallions—can be chopped ahead of time and stored in the fridge.

20-MINUTE TUSCAN TUNA NOODLES

SERVES 2 | TIME: 20 MINUTES

My mom makes a killer tuna salad. She made it often for lunch when I was young, but my brothers weren't fans so it was only consumed by Mom and me. Eventually I graduated from tuna salad (which I'll still do occasionally in a melt, hello cheese!) to plain tuna packed in olive oil. Oh my word—where was this all my life?!

I find tuna in oil so ridiculously versatile. I often throw it over salads, using the oil from the can as the dressing with a splash of vinegar. I mash it for sandwiches and toast, without having to mix in mayo or yogurt. And I adore tossing it into pasta for a super-quick and easy weeknight meal like the one below.

Kosher salt

½ pound linguine

1 tablespoon extra-virgin olive oil

1 shallot, diced

2 garlic cloves, minced

¼ teaspoon crushed red pepper flakes

Black pepper

4 cups baby spinach

1 (5-ounce) can tuna packed in oil, mostly drained

1 teaspoon freshly grated lemon zest

2 tablespoons freshly squeezed lemon juice

2 tablespoons freshly grated Parmesan cheese

3 tablespoons chopped fresh basil or parsley

Bring a pot of salted water to a boil and cook the pasta according to the package directions.

Meanwhile, heat a large skillet over medium heat and add the olive oil. Add in the shallot and garlic with the red pepper flakes and salt and black pepper to taste. Cook until the shallot is translucent, about 2 to 3 minutes. Stir in the spinach, the tuna packed in oil, and the lemon zest. Cook until the spinach wilts. Stir in the lemon juice.

Drain the pasta and add the noodles to the skillet. Toss well to combine so the noodles are coated. Add in the Parmesan and top with fresh herbs. Season with extra salt and black pepper if desired. Serve!

**10-MINUTE
MEAL PREP**

● Grate the cheese ahead of time and store it in the fridge until ready to use.

HOT HONEY SHRIMP
with smashed lime cucumber salad

SERVES 2 TO 4 | TIME: 30 MINUTES

Spicy, sweet shrimp paired with a refreshing, tangy cucumber salad is everything we need for a quick and simple dinner.

For how quickly this meal comes together, it is loaded with exceptional taste! It's so light and great for evenings when you're craving something simple but unique.

6 to 8 mini cucumbers

Kosher salt

Pinch of sugar

⅓ cup plus 2 teaspoons honey

2 jalapeño peppers, thinly sliced

1 pound jumbo shrimp, peeled and deveined

Black pepper

2 tablespoons unsalted butter

2 scallions, thinly sliced

2 tablespoons apple cider vinegar

Juice of half a lime

1 teaspoon freshly grated lime zest

Cut the cucumbers into pieces (some in half, some lengthwise, whatever you want!) and use a jar or meat tenderizer to smash each piece, gently and most of the time, just once. You can discard any seeds that come out, but place all the cucumber pieces in a large strainer. Set the strainer over a bowl. Sprinkle on a generous pinch of salt and sugar, and toss the cucumbers. If you want, you can place a bowl (or something heavy!) on top of the cucumbers to help press out the water. Let the cucumbers sit for 20 minutes at room temperature.

While the cucumbers sit, make the shrimp: In a saucepan, combine ⅓ cup of the honey and the jalapeños over medium-low heat. Let the honey come to a light simmer and then turn off the heat. Let it sit for 10 minutes. After 10 minutes, strain the honey through a fine mesh sieve to remove the jalapeños and the seeds.

Pat the shrimp dry with a paper towel and sprinkle them with salt and black pepper.

Heat a large skillet over medium heat and add the butter. Cook the shrimp for 1 to 2 minutes, then flip and cook for 1 to 2 minutes more. Drizzle in 1 to 2 tablespoons of the hot honey and cook for another 1 to 2 minutes.

Remove the shrimp and plate it. Drizzle with the remaining hot honey. Top with sliced scallions.

To make the dressing for the cucumbers: In a bowl, whisk together the vinegar, remaining 2 teaspoons of honey, and lime juice until combined.

Drain the cucumbers and place them in a large bowl. Pour on the dressing and toss well to combine. Sprinkle on the lime zest. Serve immediately with the shrimp!

10-MINUTE MEAL PREP

❶ The cucumber salad can be prepped the night before and stored in the fridge. It gets even more delicious as it sits!

HONEY DIJON PRETZEL-CRUSTED SALMON

SERVES 4 | TIME: 30 MINUTES

Coat anything in a pretzel crust and I am there.

I'm always looking for new and inventive ways to make salmon. It's not Eddie's favorite meal (he much prefers white fish or shrimp), but if I prepare it in a way that's extra good, he will relent and happily eat it for dinner.

While using just a few ingredients, this salmon has everything—massive flavor and a crunchy pretzel topping. The texture is fabulous and it pairs wonderfully with green vegetables for dinner or even potatoes and rice. It's always a huge hit at mealtime.

1 (2-pound) salmon fillet

Kosher salt and black pepper

1½ cups mini pretzel twists

2 tablespoons honey

2 tablespoons Dijon mustard

1 garlic clove, minced

2 scallions, thinly sliced

Preheat the oven to 425°F. Place the salmon on a baking sheet and sprinkle all over with salt and pepper.

Place the pretzels in a food processor or blender and pulse until small crumbs remain.

In a small bowl, stir together the honey, Dijon, and garlic until smooth. Use a spoon to brush it all over the top of the salmon. Cover with the crushed pretzels, making sure every piece of the salmon is covered with crumbs.

Bake for 12 to 15 minutes, or until the salmon is opaque and flakes easily with a fork. Sprinkle with scallions. Let cool slightly before serving.

10-MINUTE MEAL PREP

- Crush the pretzels ahead of time and store in a sealed bag in the pantry.

- Stir together the honey and Dijon and store it in the fridge.

MACADAMIA-CRUSTED SHRIMP
with apricot-chili mayo

SERVES 2 TO 4 | TIME: 30 MINUTES

This crunchy shrimp will transport you to summer nights. It tastes a little island-like and it's perfect to enjoy out on your patio. Dinner al fresco please!

If I'm being totally honest, I want to slather this apricot-chili mayo on just about everything. I love the flavor so much! And fantastic news: You can adapt this with other flavors, depending on what you have on hand. If you only have orange marmalade or fig preserves? Use that. With the exception of something like, say, blueberry jam, it's pretty darn customizable and works as a great dip.

This is a lovely dinner or snack to make for appetizers with friends.

Olive oil spray

1 pound jumbo shrimp, deveined

Kosher salt and black pepper

2 cups macadamia nuts

¼ cup almond flour

1 egg

Apricot-Chili Mayo (below)

Preheat the oven to 425°F. Line a baking sheet with a wire rack and spray the rack with olive oil spray.

Pat the shrimp completely dry with a towel. Sprinkle the shrimp with salt and pepper.

Place the nuts in a food processor and blend until small crumbs remain. Place the nuts in a dish and stir in the almond flour along with a pinch of salt and pepper. In a bowl, lightly beat the egg.

Dip each piece of shrimp in the egg and then in the crushed nut mixture. Place on the wire rack. Spritz the shrimp with olive oil spray.

Bake for 10 to 12 minutes, or until the coating is slightly golden. Serve with the apricot-chili mayo.

apricot-chili mayo

1 tablespoon apricot preserves

2 teaspoons Thai sweet chili sauce

½ cup mayonnaise

1 tablespoon chopped fresh chives

In a bowl, combine the apricot preserves, chili sauce, mayonnaise, and chives.

10-MINUTE MEAL PREP

- Crush the nuts and mix with the almond flour the day before. Store in the fridge until ready to use.

- Make the apricot-chili mayo and store it in the fridge.

SEARED SCALLOPS
with tomato cream sauce

SERVES 2 TO 4 | TIME: 30 MINUTES

These buttery, melt-in-your-mouth scallops will have you feeling like you're eating in a fancy restaurant, not your own kitchen. You'll be shocked at how quickly this meal comes together and just how wonderful it tastes.

Using fire roasted tomatoes for the tomato cream sauce adds depth of flavor without your having to cook the sauce for hours. The sauce is perfect for dipping or twirling the scallops in, and if you serve this with rice or pasta or veggies, it's wonderful on all of those, too.

Scallops cook in minutes and the brown butter adds savory, caramel-like flavor that will have you wondering why you'd ever eat scallops any other way.

1 tablespoon extra-virgin olive oil

1 shallot, diced

2 garlic cloves, minced

Kosher salt

1 tablespoon brown sugar

1 tablespoon tomato paste

½ teaspoon dried basil

½ teaspoon dried oregano

1 (14-ounce) can fire roasted tomatoes

½ cup heavy cream

2 tablespoons unsalted butter

1 pound scallops

Black pepper

Heat a pot or large skillet over medium heat and add the olive oil. Add the shallot and garlic with a pinch of salt. Cook, stirring often, until softened. Stir in the brown sugar, tomato paste, basil, and oregano. Cook for 5 minutes. Stir in the fire roasted tomatoes. Bring to a boil, then reduce to a simmer and cook for 10 minutes. Transfer to a blender and puree or use an immersion blender to smooth it out.

Pour the sauce back in the pot and heat on low. Stir in the cream. Turn off the heat.

Heat a large saucepan over medium heat and add the butter. Pat the scallops dry with a paper towel and sprinkle with salt and pepper. I like to wait until the butter just begins to brown, then add the scallops in a single layer—do not crowd the pan. You may need to work in batches. Cook the scallops for 1 to 2 minutes per side.

Serve the scallops over the tomato cream sauce, drizzling any extra brown butter from the skillet on top.

10-MINUTE MEAL PREP

❶ Make the tomato cream sauce the day before and store it in the fridge. Reheat in a saucepan over low heat until warm and creamy.

BANG BANG SALMON BURGERS

MAKES 4 BURGERS | TIME: 30 MINUTES

This recipe combines two things I love to eat: salmon and bang bang sauce! If you've never had bang bang sauce before, it's a sweet chili mayo that is heavenly.

We make salmon burgers all the time. They are SO easy to make at home and they're forgiving enough that you can add your own flavors and spices. You can prep them ahead of time, too, cooking right before you eat.

The secret to these crispy and flavorful burgers? Roll the outsides in panko bread crumbs. You get a crunchy bite on the outside that is irresistible.

And because I crave a bit more crunch, I like to make quick cabbage slaw for topping. This provides more texture and bulk to the burger, too. It's all so good!

1 (1-pound) boneless skinless salmon fillet

1 shallot, minced

2 garlic cloves, minced

1 large egg

⅓ cup seasoned bread crumbs

½ teaspoon smoked paprika

½ teaspoon kosher salt

½ teaspoon black pepper

2 tablespoons chopped fresh parsley

1 cup panko bread crumbs

4 tablespoons extra-virgin olive oil

4 buns, for serving

Bang Bang Sauce (below)

Napa Slaw recipe (page 192)

Put the salmon fillet (I cut mine into 4 pieces) to a food processor. Pulse until it is in small pieces but not completely ground up. Remove the salmon and put it in a large bowl. Add the shallot, garlic, egg, seasoned bread crumbs, smoked paprika, salt, pepper, and parsley to the bowl. Stir with a large spoon to combine, then bring the mixture together with your hands. Form the mixture into 4 burgers. (Alternatively, make 8 sliders that are slightly less than 1 inch in diameter—or however many you want so they fit the size of your buns!) Roll each burger in the panko bread crumbs.

Heat a large skillet over medium heat and add 2 tablespoons of the olive oil. Add 2 of the burgers and cook on both sides until golden brown, about 2 to 3 minutes per side. You want the insides of the burgers to be opaque, so I usually turn the heat down to low and cover the skillet for another minute or two after the second side has browned to ensure that they are cooked. Remove from the pan and repeat with the remaining olive oil and burgers.

To assemble, place each burger on a bun and top with bang bang sauce and slaw.

10-MINUTE MEAL PREP

❶ Burgers can be formed ahead of time and stored in the fridge for up to 2 days. They can also be stored in the freezer, individually wrapped in plastic wrap, for up to 3 months.

❷ Bang bang sauce can be made ahead and stored in the fridge.

bang bang sauce

½ cup mayonnaise

2 tablespoons Thai sweet chili sauce

1 teaspoon sriracha

In a small bowl, whisk together the mayonnaise, chili sauce, and sriracha.

SMOKY CHIPOTLE BEER-BATTERED HALIBUT TACOS

SERVES 3 OR 4 | TIME: 30 MINUTES

My dad started making a quick beer-battered fish when I was a kid and ever since, I've been hooked. This recipe does not require deep-frying the fish—instead, a quick pan-fry yields a light, lovely breading.

You can use most varieties of white fish here with success. I love the smoky flavor that the spices add, but in a pinch, plain flour, salt, and pepper work great with the beer.

The general rule of tacos applies: What do you enjoy stuffed inside a tortilla? When it comes to fish tacos, shredded cabbage or vinegary slaw is a must for me. The quick pickled cabbage is marinated and wonderful—it's soft with a slight crunch and adds a delicious briny flavor. Lime adds brightness and avocado brings creaminess to the taco.

Quick Pickled Red Cabbage (page 35), optional

1½ cups all-purpose flour

1 teaspoon garlic powder

1 teaspoon onion powder

½ teaspoon smoked paprika

½ teaspoon kosher salt

½ teaspoon ground chipotle chile powder

10 ounces of your favorite beer

¼ cup canola, vegetable, or olive oil, plus more as needed

2 pounds halibut, cut into pieces

8 (4-inch) flour tortillas

1 or 2 avocados, thinly sliced

Chipotle Crema (page 46), for serving

Crumbled cotija cheese, for serving

Chopped fresh cilantro, for serving

If serving with the pickled cabbage, make that first so it can sit while you make the tacos.

In a bowl, combine the flour, garlic powder, onion powder, smoked paprika, salt, and chile powder and whisk to combine. Pour in the beer and whisk until a smooth batter forms.

Heat a large nonstick skillet over medium-high heat and add the oil. Dip the fish in the batter and coat it completely, then drop it in the skillet to fry. Let each piece of fish fry until the sides appear golden and crispy, about 3 to 4 minutes per side. Gently remove the pieces with a spatula and place them on a paper towel to absorb any liquid. Repeat with all the fish, adding more oil if needed.

To make the fish tacos, place the tortillas on a work surface and layer with the fish and avocado. Drizzle with the chipotle crema and top with the pickled red cabbage (if using), cotija, and cilantro. Serve!

10-MINUTE MEAL PREP

- The pickled cabbage can be made ahead of time and stored in the fridge.
- The crema can be made ahead of time and stored in the fridge.

SIDE

DISHES

By now you know that my mom was the queen of the weeknight meal. She made a main dish and at least two sides, along with some sort of bread, even if it was straight from the freezer or bakery-bought sliced Italian bread with butter.

I never thought much about how she put together complete meals and it wasn't until I married Eddie—who absolutely lives for side dishes—that I put an emphasis on creating full meals. The question I receive most often from you is, "But what side dish should I serve with that?" and I'm hoping this section gives you a few no-fail ideas. These are our favorite sides that truly go with most meals and don't take that long to make. Plus, if you chop and prep your veggies at the beginning of the week, these come together in no time!

THE HOUSE SALAD THAT GOES WITH EVERYTHING

SERVES 4 | TIME: 30 MINUTES

This is it: The salad that truly does go with everything. It's been my house salad for years now. It's simple but classic. The croutons really make it. And when drizzled with the house vinaigrette, it takes on so much flavor!

SOURDOUGH CROUTONS

2 cups torn sourdough bread pieces or cubes

2 tablespoons extra-virgin olive oil

1 teaspoon garlic powder

¼ teaspoon kosher salt

SALAD

12 ounces fresh spring greens, baby lettuce, or greens of choice

Kosher salt and black pepper

1 pint grape tomatoes, halved

1 bell pepper, diced

1 small shallot, diced

⅓ cup jarred mild banana peppers, drained

⅓ cup freshly grated Parmesan cheese

¼ cup roasted, salted sunflower seeds

House Vinaigrette (page 58)

To make the croutons: Preheat the oven to 400°F. Spread the bread pieces on a baking sheet and drizzle with the olive oil, tossing well. Sprinkle with the garlic powder and salt, tossing again. Bake for 15 to 20 minutes, or until golden and crisp.

To make the salad: Add your greens to a large bowl and season them liberally with salt and black pepper. Add the tomatoes, bell pepper, shallot, banana peppers, Parmesan, sunflower seeds, and croutons. Toss with the house vinaigrette and serve!

10-MINUTE MEAL PREP

❶ Make the croutons 24 hours ahead of time and store them in a resealable bag at room temperature.

❷ Chop the vegetables 24 hours ahead of time and store together in the fridge.

❸ Make the dressing ahead of time and store in the fridge.

MY SECRET TO PERFECT ROASTED VEGETABLES EVERY TIME

SERVES 2 | TIME: 30 MINUTES

Roasting is 100 percent the reason behind my love of vegetables. I started roasting vegetables every darn day and it just flipped a switch: I was going to eat them.

This recipe applies to veggies of all textures and thicknesses, and I find that roasting them at 425°F is the key. One veggie may need a bit longer than another, but as long as you don't crowd the pan, they should end up perfectly crisp!

2 to 3 cups chopped vegetables (such as broccoli, Brussels sprouts, squash, potatoes, carrots, and peppers, just to name a few)

1 tablespoon extra-virgin olive oil

½ teaspoon kosher salt

½ teaspoon freshly cracked black pepper

½ teaspoon garlic powder

Preheat the oven to 425°F.

Place the vegetables on one or two baking sheets, making sure that you don't crowd the pan. Drizzle the veggies with olive oil. Season with the salt, pepper, and garlic powder and toss to combine.

Roast anywhere from 15 to 25 minutes, flipping once or twice during cook time.

10-MINUTE MEAL PREP _____

➊ I'm a broken record, but chop your vegetables ahead of time and store them in the fridge!

MY MOM'S SIMPLE TOMATO SALAD

SERVES 2 TO 4 | TIME: 15 MINUTES

Pennsylvania tomatoes are heartbreaking. Until they aren't. For most of the year, they are barely edible—until you reach the sweet spot of midsummer. And then? Well, then they absolutely blow your mind. You forgive them for being hard, orange rocks in previous months or for disappearing completely. For two to three months, you forget how they did you dirty and envelop yourself in complete and utter lust.

Before the beautiful caprese salads of social media became a thing, my mom was the tomato salad queen. We're talking at least twenty years back. Nearly every single summer night with dinner, she would slice homegrown tomatoes and drizzle them with balsamic vinegar. Then she'd add a sprinkle of Gorgonzola cheese—one of her and my dad's favorites.

This is a classic salad that goes with any dinner but tastes best in summertime. Make a big platter for a cookout or slice one tomato and eat it with your meal. You won't even miss the mozzarella!

2 homegrown tomatoes, sliced ¼ inch thick

½ teaspoon kosher salt

½ teaspoon freshly cracked black pepper

¼ cup crumbled Gorgonzola

Balsamic Vinaigrette (page 52)

Fresh herbs or microgreens, for garnish

Place the tomatoes on a platter and sprinkle them with the salt and pepper. Crumble on the Gorgonzola and then drizzle with the vinaigrette. Garnish with fresh herbs or microgreens. Serve immediately.

10-MINUTE MEAL PREP _____

➊ Make the balsamic vinaigrette ahead of time and store it in the fridge.

ROASTED CABBAGE WEDGES
with garlic oil and lemon

SERVES 2 TO 4 | TIME: 30 MINUTES

If you haven't tried roasted cabbage yet, get ready to have your mind blown. The cabbage edges get crispy and caramelly, golden and browned, and if you use the garlic oil . . . the flavor is life-changing. This is a side that can truly go with almost any dish. We adore it!

1 head green cabbage, cut into wedges

2 tablespoons garlic olive oil, from the Garlic Confit (page 36)

Kosher salt and black pepper

Pinch of crushed red pepper flakes

1 lemon, cut into wedges

Preheat the oven to 425°F. Place the cabbage wedges on a baking sheet.

Brush the cabbage with the garlic olive oil and sprinkle with salt, black pepper, and red pepper flakes. Roast for 20 to 25 minutes, flipping once during cook time, until golden and caramelly.

Remove from the oven and spritz with lemon. Serve immediately.

10-MINUTE MEAL PREP

- Prep the garlic confit ahead of time and store it in the fridge.

PARMESAN ROASTED BROCCOLI

SERVES 4 | TIME: 25 MINUTES

This roasted broccoli is my ideal way to eat broccoli. This is a side dish that everyone loves—it's roasted to perfection, nutty, slightly cheesy, and all around loaded with flavor. It's an easy go-to side dish for weeknights, but it also makes a great addition to pasta or rice.

I often use the leftovers in grain bowls (page 91), on top of salads, or even stirred into scrambled eggs.

It's perfection!

Nonstick cooking spray

2 heads broccoli, cut into florets

2 tablespoons extra-virgn olive oil

¼ cup raw, unsalted pine nuts

½ teaspoon kosher salt

½ teaspoon freshly cracked black pepper

2 to 3 tablespoons freshly grated Parmesan cheese

Preheat the oven to 425°F. Line a baking sheet with foil and spray with nonstick spray.

Place the broccoli on the sheet and drizzle with the olive oil. Cover with the pine nuts, salt, pepper, and Parmesan.

Roast for 20 to 25 minutes, or until the broccoli is golden brown and the pine nuts are toasted. Check halfway through, as the pine nuts may start to burn—you want to keep an eye on it and toss the mixture if needed.

Remove from the oven and sprinkle with more Parmesan if desired. Serve immediately.

10-MINUTE MEAL PREP

❶ Chop the broccoli ahead of time and store it in the fridge.

GARLIC + CHIVE BUTTER SMASHED POTATOES

SERVES 2 TO 4 | TIME: 45 MINUTES

It's easy to say that smashed potatoes are the most popular side dish in our kitchen. They are Eddie's favorite, winning by a landslide. The kids love them. They go with virtually anything. And you can add so many flavors to them, based on what you serve them with!

— You can do dried or fresh herbs.

— Make a dip or drizzle sauce for them.

— Top them with cheese or hummus.

— Use them as a base for eggs.

Seriously, the options are endless! And in all honesty—I could eat a plate of these for a meal.

This dish takes a bit longer than our usual 30 minutes. But most of it is hands-off time: hands-off while boiling the potatoes and hands-off while roasting. And the good news is that if you boil the potatoes ahead of time as meal prep, this dish will actually only take 30 minutes.

These potatoes are crispy and crunchy and absolutely worth it.

2 pounds baby Yukon Gold potatoes

2 tablespoons extra-virgin olive oil

½ teaspoon kosher salt

½ teaspoon freshly cracked black pepper

4 tablespoons unsalted butter

2 garlic cloves, minced

2 tablespoons chopped fresh chives

Place the potatoes in a large pot and fill it with cold water. Bring the water to a boil. Simmer the potatoes until they are just barely fork-tender, about 10 minutes. Strain the potatoes and let them cool slightly.

Preheat the oven to 450°F.

Brush a baking sheet with 1 tablespoon of olive oil. Place the potatoes on the sheet. Use your hand or the bottom of a small glass to smash them down, trying to keep them in one piece.

Drizzle the remaining tablespoon of olive oil over the potatoes. Sprinkle the potatoes with the salt and pepper.

Place the sheet in the oven and roast the potatoes for 25 to 30 minutes, until golden and crispy.

10-MINUTE MEAL PREP

❶ Boil the potatoes, then let them cool completely. Store them in a sealed container or bag in the fridge for up to 3 days until you're ready to use.

While the potatoes are roasting, make the garlic chive butter: In a small saucepan, melt the butter over medium heat. Once melted, stir in the garlic and chives. Turn off the heat.

Remove the potatoes from the oven and brush with the garlic chive butter. Serve immediately.

SMASHED CHILI SWEET POTATOES

SERVES 2 TO 4 | TIME: 45 MINUTES

These are similar to the crispy smashed potatoes (see page 249) that we make all the time, but I'm giving you a sweet potato option! We love these with extra spice, so I like to add new flavors and use cheese. If you're a sweet potato purist, you can absolutely make these with salt, pepper, and a bit of garlic! If you're feeling freaky, you can drizzle on some maple syrup and top with a hint of almond butter after roasting.

Truly, the options are endless! While I share my favorite flavor combination below, I encourage you to make this recipe your own and use what you can find in your fridge and pantry.

The key here is to make sure you cut your potatoes into thirds (if they are medium size). You want them to be easily "smashable" so those edges get crispy and delish!

2 to 3 pounds sweet potatoes

3 tablespoons extra-virgin olive oil

½ teaspoon kosher salt

½ teaspoon freshly cracked black pepper

½ teaspoon garlic powder

¼ teaspoon chili powder

1 tablespoon chili garlic sauce (optional)

2 tablespoons crumbled feta cheese

2 tablespoons chopped fresh herbs, like cilantro or parsley

Cut the potatoes in thirds. I like to leave the skin on, but feel free to peel them!

Preheat the oven to 450°F.

Place the potatoes in a large pot and fill it with cold water. Bring the water to a boil. Simmer the potatoes until they are just barely fork-tender, about 15 minutes. Strain the potatoes and let them cool slightly.

Brush a baking sheet with 1½ tablespoons of olive oil. Place the potatoes on the sheet. Use your hand or the bottom of a small glass to push them down gently. Try to keep them in one piece.

Drizzle the remaining 1½ tablespoons of olive oil over the potatoes. Stir together the salt, pepper, garlic powder, and chili powder. Sprinkle it over the potatoes.

Place the baking sheet in the oven and roast the potatoes for 25 to 30 minutes, until golden and crispy.

Remove and drizzle with the chili garlic sauce if you like things spicy. Top with a crumbling of feta cheese and herbs. Serve immediately.

10-MINUTE MEAL PREP

❶ Boil the potatoes, then let them cool completely. Store them in a sealed container or bag in the fridge until you're ready to use.

FRESH GREEN BEAN SALAD

SERVES 2 TO 4 | TIME: 30 MINUTES

This crisp green bean salad is one of my favorite summer dishes. The green beans are super crunchy and fresh and the dressing is tangy and rich. You top it all with walnuts and crumbled feta. I could eat a whole bowl of it for lunch!

And P.S. If you're not into feta or goat cheese, you can sub in Parmesan.

1 pound fresh green beans

¼ cup freshly squeezed lemon juice

2 tablespoons Dijon mustard

½ cup extra-virgin olive oil

Kosher salt and freshly cracked black pepper

1 tablespoon chopped fresh chives

⅓ cup crumbled feta or goat cheese

⅓ cup toasted walnuts, chopped

Prepare an ice bath: Fill a large bowl with ice and cold water.

Bring a large pot of water to a boil. Once boiling, add the green beans and cook for 3 to 4 minutes. Use a strainer to immediately transfer the beans to the ice bath. Let them chill in the bath for 5 minutes. Pat the beans dry with a paper towel

In a bowl, whisk together the lemon juice and mustard. Whisk in the oil until the dressing is emulsified. Add a pinch of salt and pepper along with the chives. Whisk to combine.

Place the beans on a plate and give them a light sprinkle of salt and pepper. Drizzle on the Dijon dressing. Top with the crumbled feta and walnuts. Serve immediately.

10-MINUTE MEAL PREP

- Blanch the green beans ahead of time and store them in the fridge.
- Chop and toast the walnuts ahead of time and store in the pantry.
- Make the dressing and store it in the fridge. Shake before using.

CURRY ROASTED CAULIFLOWER
with brown butter and crispy capers

SERVES 2 TO 4 | TIME: 25 MINUTES

Years ago, cookbook author Heidi Swanson turned me on to the beauty of curried brown butter. It's since become a staple concoction in my kitchen and is fabulous drizzled on soups or breads.

Here we're making things easier: Simply toss the cauliflower with the spices and melted butter. The butter will brown in the oven and the flavors will come together beautifully.

The best part of this recipe?? Crispy capers! These add texture and tartness. If you're anything like me and live for briny flavors, you may eat them by the spoonful.

1 head cauliflower, cut into florets

4 tablespoons unsalted butter, melted

½ teaspoon kosher salt

½ teaspoon freshly ground black pepper

½ teaspoon curry powder

1 teaspoon extra-virgin olive oil

¼ cup capers, drained and patted completely dry

Preheat the oven to 425°F.

Place the florets on a baking sheet. Drizzle with the melted butter. Toss so all of the cauliflower is covered. Sprinkle with the salt, pepper, and curry powder. Toss again so everything is combined.

Roast for 15 to 20 minutes, tossing occasionally, until the cauliflower is golden and the butter is browned.

Meanwhile, heat a small skillet over medium-high heat and add the olive oil. Add the dry capers and shake the pan or stir, tossing for 1 to 2 minutes, until crispy and fried. Remove the capers and place on a paper towel until ready to use.

Remove the cauliflower from the oven and cover with the crispy capers! Serve immediately.

10-MINUTE MEAL PREP

❶ Cut the cauliflower into florets and store it in the fridge until ready to use.

COCONUT ROASTED CARROTS

SERVES 2 TO 4 | TIME: 30 MINUTES

Roasted carrots are my new BFF. If I'm being totally honest, the classic carrot is a veggie that I just couldn't gravitate toward. It's ridiculous, given that carrots are sweet and usually a kid favorite. Plus, their dipping capabilities are out of this world. And I never pass up a good dip.

Roasting carrots changed the way I look at these orange beauties. They become caramelly and sweet. When tossed with shredded coconut, they become toasty and golden. It's the perfect mix of sweet and savory and a great dish for someone who is new to carrot love.

½ pound carrots, peeled and cut into 2-inch pieces

1 tablespoon coconut oil, melted

½ teaspoon kosher salt

½ teaspoon freshly cracked black pepper

1 tablespoon shredded unsweetened coconut

Preheat the oven to 425°F.

In a bowl, toss the carrots with the coconut oil, salt, and pepper. Spread them in a single layer on a baking sheet and roast for 15 minutes. Sprinkle on the shredded coconut and toss well. Roast for 10 minutes more.

Serve immediately.

10-MINUTE MEAL PREP

❶ Wash, peel, and cut your carrots to prep them for roasting. Store in a container or a bag in the fridge until you're ready to use.

NOTE

These are also amazing with the Five-Minute Marcona Almond Granola (page 70) sprinkled on top!

CHIPOTLE, BACON, BLUE CHEESE BRUSSELS SPROUTS

SERVES 2 TO 4 | TIME: 30 MINUTES

I cannot get enough of the chipotle–blue cheese combo. It's spicy and flavorful while also being tangy and creamy at the same time. Meanwhile, the roasted Brussels sprouts are charred and toasty. Divine!

8 slices thick-cut bacon, chopped

1 pound Brussels sprouts, stems removed and quartered

1 tablespoon extra-virgin olive oil

1 tablespoon brown sugar

1 teaspoon ground chipotle chile powder

½ teaspoon freshly cracked black pepper

½ teaspoon garlic powder

½ cup crumbled blue cheese

Preheat the oven to 425°F.

Heat a skillet over medium heat and add the bacon. Cook until some of the fat has rendered but the bacon is not yet crispy.

Place the Brussels sprouts in a bowl. Drizzle the bacon and any fat in the skillet over the sprouts. Add the olive oil. Stir together the brown sugar, chipotle powder, pepper, and garlic powder. Sprinkle it over the sprouts and toss until everything is combined.

Spread the sprouts and bacon mixture out on a baking sheet. Roast for 15 to 20 minutes, tossing once or twice. Remove from the oven and cover with blue cheese. Let sit for 5 minutes before serving.

10-MINUTE MEAL PREP

- Trim and chop the Brussels sprouts ahead of time and store them in the fridge.

- Stir together the spices and store in the pantry.

BEST EVER GARLIC BREAD

SERVES 4 TO 6 | TIME: 25 MINUTES

Now that I've convinced you to fall in love with garlic confit, you hold the secret to making the best garlic bread . . . ever. Truly!

This bread is baked with that golden, caramelized garlic, which becomes even more flavorful in the oven. It's salty with a hint of Parmesan. It's buttery and toasty. It has a hint of freshness from the herbs that makes you feel like it's summer all year long.

It's hard to tell you how many people this will serve because it's quite irresistible. Before you know it, you're on your second slice. It's fabulous for dipping in sauce or even more garlic oil, but also absolutely incredible on its own.

½ cup unsalted butter, softened

6 garlic cloves from Garlic Confit (page 36), mashed

2 tablespoons freshly grated Parmesan cheese

½ teaspoon kosher salt

1 loaf of your favorite ciabatta bread or baguette

2 tablespoons oil from Garlic Confit (page 36)

3 tablespoons chopped fresh basil

Preheat the oven to 400°F.

In a bowl, stir together the butter, mashed garlic cloves, Parmesan, and salt.

Slice the bread down the center. Spread the garlic butter on the cut sides of the bread. Drizzle the bread with the garlic oil.

Place on a baking sheet and bake for 15 minutes or until golden and crispy. Sprinkle with fresh basil and serve.

**10-MINUTE
MEAL PREP**

- Spread the garlic butter on the bread and wrap the bread in foil. Store it in the fridge for up to 12 hours until you're ready to drizzle with oil and bake. You may need to add 1 to 2 minutes to the bake time if baking this straight from the fridge.

acknowledgments

To the readers of *How Sweet Eats*, thank you so very much for making my dreams come true. None of this would be possible without your support and encouragement over the last twelve years! Thank you for making my recipes, sharing them with your friends and family, and inspiring me every day.

Stacey, thank you for being a rock-star agent and friend for all these years!

Dervla, I still can't believe I have the privilege to work with you. You are my dream editor and I'm so thankful you have believed in me for such a long time. Thank you for reading through all of my words (we know there are way too many) and believing in me.

Thank you to Katherine, Christina, Brianne, Serena, Mia, Jessica, Kim, and the entire team at Penguin Random House for the countless hours of work that went into bringing this book together.

Thank you to all of my wonderful recipe testers, especially Molly and Kat, who helped these recipes come to life.

Erin, thank you so much for your incredible help in styling this book. Working with you is the most fun!

Alex, none of this would be possible without you. I have no words.

Lacy, I can't even begin to thank you for all the work you did to make this book happen! You are my lifelong BFF, my sister forever, and the person I get the most inspiration from. *How Sweet Eats* is what it is because of you!

Mom and Dad, thank you for your dedication to making sure we sat around the table and ate dinner together every single night when I was kid. Even if it was 9 PM.

Eddie, Max, and Emilia, oh I love you so much! And Eddie, thanks for happily eating reheated leftovers for almost an entire year as I tested recipes for the book. You are my muse!

index

ABOUT THE AUTHOR

Jessica Merchant is a full-time recipe developer and writer
who happens to be crazy passionate about all things food.
She is the author of *The Pretty Dish* and *Seriously Delish*,
and details her adventures in and out of the kitchen on her
popular blog, *How Sweet Eats*, which is read by millions.
She lives in Pittsburgh, Pennsylvania, with her family.